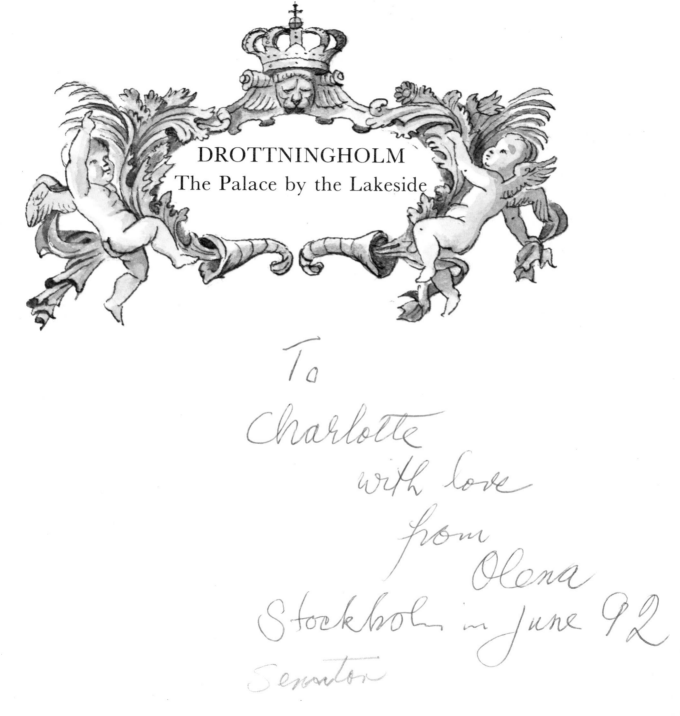

DROTTNINGHOLM
The Palace by the Lakeside

To

Charlotte

with love

from

Olena

Stockholm in June 92

Senator

Jan Mårtenson

DROTTNINGHOLM
The Palace by the Lakeside

ILLUSTRATED BY

Gunnar Brusewitz

Translated from the Swedish by Eric Dickens

WAHLSTRÖM & WIDSTRAND

Printed in Italy, 1985
ISBN 91-46-14939-2

For Ingrid

"Drottningholm, thy splendour enchants"
Carl Michael Bellman

Preface

This book is an account of an old love affair, the story of "my" Drottningholm. It is not an attempt to be a thesis in the History of Art, nor a tourist guidebook. Instead, I have strolled through the landscape of time and stopped to consider that which has taken my fancy. The meetings with the complex genius of Gustav III. The Chinese Pavilion, the epitome of Swedish Rococo where the step was taken from the stiff, gilt leather of the Baroque towards the pleasantly soft silk of the Rococo. The white marble statues in the park, the flickering candles of the Court Theatre where impulses from the world beyond the Spruce Curtain flared up like glittering fans.

Gunnar Brusewitz has illustrated my wanderings through cultural history just as in our book "Utsikt från min trappa". Using restrained resources and seemingly without effort, he masterly captures with great skill an epoch, an era, an atmosphere.

I owe warm thanks to Dr Stig Fogelmarck the Chief and Dr Göran Alm as well as Baron Carl-Fredrik Palmstierna, Curator of the Royal Art Collections, for their valuable opinions and comments.

New York, spring 1984

Jan Mårtenson

The Heart of Sweden

I am sitting on a early-morning train on the way to New York looking out of the window at the tired, threadbare cityscape and thinking of Sweden. What does your native land mean to you when you are far away? What does the very concept mean? In which Sweden do you have your roots? Not those practical, professional roots but the ones belonging to your emotions. In the land of childhood, sunlit among the wild strawberry patches of holiday time, the land of lilacs at the end of the summer term where the green palms of water-lilies float on dark waters? Or do the December days when snow falls silently mean more, or the shiny reflections in the city asphalt after autumn rains in the evenings?

For me, places and moods are important points of reference. Verner von Heidenstam, the Nobel Prize laureate in Literature who lived abroad for long stretches at a time, crystallised his feelings in his "five lines", a poem ending with the verse "I long for the stones, where I, a child, played". The stones in question are to be found in the dark green wilderness of Tiveden, near Olshammar, where he was born "among the ring of hammer-blows and the soughing of the trees". Carl von Linné compressed the same thoughts into two words: "Nostalgia-Stenbrohult." By now old, tired and sick, he wrote these words in his sprawling handwriting shortly before he died, far away from the lilies of the valley, the call of the cuckoo on bright May nights by the little rector's house in Småland where he was born. Many more have come to the same conclusion, that it is ultimately not the people we have known but the landscape, the countryside that we feel nostalgia towards, the land that moulded us right from the start.

At a distance of thousands of miles it is difficult to give a universal answer to the question as to what that the concept of native land means, but for me Sweden can be summed up in Drottningholm park an early morning in June. The mist lifts off the waters with the first breeze, as from silk. The water grows ever bluer as it takes up the hue of the heavens. Like a herd of silvery-grey bull elephants the oaks graze in the pale green succulent grass. A mass of cowslips has followed in the wake of the blue and purple occupation of hepatica on the hillside near the Chinese Pavilion. From the island of Kersö the rhythmic call of a cuckoo can be heard, while a drake, its head exhibiting that characteristic metallic sheen, is paddling down by the bathing pavilion. And from the tall alders planted close together come snatches of the folk-music of a blackbird.

I am standing on one of the avenues of lime-trees listening to the faint bubbling of water from the spring in the Baroque Garden which lies in front of the sleeping Palace. It is here that Sweden begins for me; perhaps it also ends here. Why is this? There are, of course, as many images of Sweden as there are people who think about it. Stockholm would be the most logical heart of Sweden: commercial centre, seat of government, gateway to Lake Mälaren and the rich expanses beyond. The Old Town, Gamla Stan, where pomp and circumstance, mundanity and bloody dramas have followed close on one another, through the ages. The town square, Stortorget, where the final act in the cruel Renaissance spectacle, the Bloodbath of Stockholm, took place when "blood ran mixed with rainwater" as heads rolled under the executioner's sword of the Danish King, Christian. One evening under the oaks on the island of Djurgården. The vista of sea and sky from Västerbro bridge. An early morning walk through the silent city, snow that falls over Biblioteksgatan.

Or, and why not, Gamla Uppsala with its royal burial mounds, if it is an historical point of departure you are looking for when forming your image of Sweden. The ancient tree of the Norns, the Goddesses of Fate, the ash, grew there. Of Urd, Skuld and Verdandi. The roots may still lie under the green grassy banks surrounding the small stone church which was built right over the foundations of Woden's temple. Perhaps this is a truer location for the heart of Sweden?

But for me it is Drottningholm. And to my subjective imagination there is at least one objective aspect. Lovön, the island on which Drottningholm is situated, is one of the sites around Lake Mälaren where the greatest number of archeological treasures have been disco-

"Trees full shadowy outstretching", sang Bellman when describing the park at Drottningholm.

vered. Access to the fertile Mälar Valley, the heart of what was to become Sweden and the area where four capitals had been built, was controlled at this point. The waterways were the road into the interior when coming from the world of the sea. Ice Age ridges which run at right angles to the Mälar Valley eased communications to the north and south.

During the Middle Ages Lovön was called "Logho" i.e. isle of *logh*. This name is incorporated in the old name for Lake Mälaren, which in the works of Snorri Sturlúson was called "Loginn".

"The famous Lake Mälaren, which divides the three splendid Provinces of the Kingdom of Sweden, Upland, Södermannelander and Vestmanneland" has an interesting, if not necessarily historically accurate, history. King Gylfi promised the Norse goddess Gefjun a piece of land the compass of which she could plough in a single day. With her four sons as oxen she ploughed herself a tract of land that she lifted up and set down in the sea where it became the Danish island of Zealand. The hole left behind became Lake Mälaren.

Nearby lies the island of Helgö, a proof in itself of the widespread nature of trade contacts with its advanced production of gold, silver, bronze and iron. The thousands of archeological discoveries on Helgö have shown it to be of real significance as the central area of Sweden. "The historical and scientific value of the discoveries can hardly be exaggerated" say the archeologists. Not only workshops, casting-moulds and gold leaf. Also Roman coins, a British bishop's crozier from the 8th century and a Buddha statue from India, that is even older. Were they brought home by the Viking fleets with their bearded

11

farmers at the oars, men who had exchanged winters of sitting around the hearths of their cottages for the salt of the sea and long expeditions? Or were these objects obtained by means of the growing amount of peaceful trading? A little further away lies Birka where St. Anskar was sent by the Emperor Louis to preach God's word to the heathens.

After the mediaeval Wars of Union and other unrest, Gustav Vasa stepped out of the anonymity of history and laid his authoritative hand on Lovön. He obtained by barter Glia village which lay where Gustav III was to build his Gothic Tower, and incorporated several manors to form Torvesund Royal Estate. Gustavus Vasa's captain, Peter Fredag, was stationed near Glia during the siege of Stockholm in 1521 when the city was occupied by King Christian of Denmark. On Christmas Eve the Danes sailed out of Stockholm. The winter was mild and the sea free of ice. They came with forty boats and small craft to battle with Peter Fredag who controlled the gateway to Lake Mälaren. They

The Palace of the Queen Dowager

aimed to "visit Peter Fredag and have a taste of his yule barrel". But it is told that Fredag stationed sixteen of his men with hunting horns in the hills round about. When the Danes landed they heard how the call to arms sounded from all quarters. Peder Fredag's troops, though inferior in numbers, attacked the Danes, whose morale had been broken, and they fled in panic. "Two hundred Danes fell on the spot, more perished in the water into which they plunged, horse, harness and all. The rest in their confusion fled towards the boats and arrived bloody and badly wounded, their mission a failure, back in Stockholm in a state of great distress."

Gustav Vasa was succeeded by his son Johan III, who built the first palace at the end of the 16th Century. He gave the palace to his queen, Katarina Jagiellonica, and named it Drottningholm (i.e. Queen's Isle) after her. His palace burnt down one cold December day in 1661, but a new palace was soon built on the site of the old one, an expression of great political might, a Baroque palace built by the Queen Dowager, Hedvig Eleonora. Other queens followed suit. Lovisa Ulrica, sister of Frederick the Great of Prussia, received the palace as a wedding present in 1744, when she married the heir to the throne, Adolf Fredrik. Her strong character, her intelligence and education, instilled in her by such men as Voltaire, at the brilliant court at Potsdam, were of key importance for the development of Swedish culture and of Drottningholm itself. There she founded the Academy of Learning and her passionate interest in things theatrical led to the building of the Court Theatre. Lovisa Ulrica's art collection became one of the corner-stones of the National Museum and she made additions to the Palace, softening its style with Rococo features. With her, the rigidity of the Baroque was superseded by the pleasant soft silk of the Rococo.

Her son, Gustav III, took over Drottningholm in 1777. He waved the magic wand of his esprit over the park, adding lace cuffs to the homespun culture of Sweden. The theatre was embellished by the grace of the King and a poor man's Versailles arose among fir trees and spruce. He set out the English Park, and the white marble statues against a background of dark green are his creation. The park grew out of marshy ground which had, in former times made Drottningholm "so unhealthy that the strongest constitution was broken there, so that the fevers and autumn ague of Drottningholm were rife, and notorious for their acute nature".

The sister-in-law to the King, Hedvig Charlotte, describes life at Drottningholm in her diaries: "Life at Drottningholm is rather strange, a cross between town and country life, unlike anything else, a combination of courtly pleasures and country pastimes, of etiquette and freedom, of jollity and seclusion".

But the brilliant Gustavian era at Drottningholm was soon to come to an abrupt end. A shot fired at a masked ball cut short the hectic

The "real" way, the oldest way of arriving at Drottningholm is by boat.

theatrical life of Gustav III.

And one pale March, many years later, his son was imprisoned there following the bloodless coup in the city of Stockholm. Finland had fallen, the army had revolted and exile awaited.

Yet the idyll was to return. Oscar I lived here with his Consort, Joséphine, and on her namesday in August, inhabitants of Stockholm made the journey out to Drottningholm with their hampers and victuals, fireworks were set off, people sang and cheered. Black plumes of smoke drifted in from white steamers towards the Palace, people strolled along the gravel paths. The years flowed peacefully on under the tops of the lime trees. A belovèd and well-esteemed Gustav VI Adolf lived there and it is here that Sweden's present King and Queen have moved.

Too much emphasis should perhaps not be placed on lists of kings and queens and royal houses, but it cannot be denied that these are a practical aid to memory. Dramatic and significant events in history are often connected with the leading figures of the time. As regards Drottningholm, the association is even greater. Every owner has left his or her personal touch on the palace.

15

As I stand in the park, I can see how the blue and yellow pennant on the roof of the Palace flutters in the morning breeze and I can smell the sweetness of the flowering lime trees. I feel I am standing at a timeless geometric centre. Here my Sweden focusses most sharply, here is the point of intersection. A literary, architectonic and cultural intersection.

In the distance, among the trees, the Court Theatre can be seen behind the white statue of the Apollo Belvedere representing the Sun God. The original can be found in the Vatican. A Greek god in marble in front of the austere façade of the Theatre, this too with its roots in Greek culture. It is one of the best preserved 18th Century theatres in the world with unique décor and stage settings. The repertoire is much the same as when the Theatre, created by Lovisa Ulrica and Gustav III, was one of the gateways to French culture. From the flies, the "gloire" is lowered, the cloud with Rococo gods and goddesses, just as it was two hundred years before. Underneath, in the basement lies the Theatre's own surrealistic landscape with pullies, ropes and timbers like an old sailing ship. Here new impressions opened up a world beyond the edge of the pine forest. Impressions like fans against the greyness of an impoverished Sweden.

The gentle bubbling sound of water coming from behind my back is from Hercules fountain in the Baroque Garden. The group of statues was booty from Wallenstein's palace in Prague with additions from Fredriksborg Castle in Denmark. They are trophies, green with verdegris, from the days when Sweden was a great power, plundering and laying waste the cities and villages of Europe.

Further away, beyond Flora Rise, the Chinese Pavilion can be seen. A cake-like, Rococo creation in pastel pink, an item of chinoiserie with sumptuous furnishings, originally built in secret as a *maison de plaisance*, a *surprise* by Adolf Fredrik during the summer of 1753 for Lovisa Ulrica on her birthday.

And beyond the China Pavilion lies Canton, another idyll. Lovisa Ulrica wanted to create a "pre-industrial" society in the 18th Century houses. In line with the optimistic mercantilism of the Period of Liberty, where import was to be replaced by self-sufficiency and export, she started a manufactory for the production of silk stockings, a silk farm and a lace-making school with lace-makers from Brabant as instructors. Mulberry bushes were planted in a spirit of confidence in what the future would bring and silkworms were bred to produce the silk. That which remains today is a charming reminiscence of well-preserved 18th Century. But it remains a mere ripple in the long history of silk manufacture.

This side of Canton, in the depths of the Baroque Garden, Castor and Pollux shine brightly in marble among the dark green foliage. This group of statues Gustav III had erected in the romantic English Park. The star-shaped boscage in front, originally an arrangement of bushy hedges in Baroque style, has now become a grove of tall trees. The eight paths still form a star, but the trees have grown into tall straight pillars. A cathedral with foliage as its roof and the wind as distant organ music.

Gravel crunches beneath my feet as I walk along the row of cascades. In former times, water was supplied by means of hollowed-out tree trunks. Up by the ponds, across the fields Mars shines whitely and in the distance we can see the Governor's Residence standing among Iron Age graves. The Swedish era of the Vikings, Ancient Rome. Monuments in stone and above, the summer sky arches while a lark hovers high over the Fountain of Hercules.

I look towards the Palace. When is it at its best? Now, an early summer's morning in June? Or a moonlit night in August with a shimmer of unreality over the white marble statues and the pale yellow façade of the Palace as the shadows grow ever more deep? Or on a crisp winter's day when the sun glistens on the snow and the ice crystals and every line of these austere buildings stands out in the logical simplicity of beauty? But it is perhaps autumn that gives us more, the season of the Baroque. The tops of the trees are almost stripped of their former abundance. Through the graphical simplicity of the trunks, the linear façades appear. When I descend into the park, through the gate with Hedvig Eleonora's gilt monogram complete with crown, the leaves lie golden in the avenue of limes. The vista, looking into the distance, seems endless. Under a grey sky the wind carries the music of the composer Johan Roman. His composition for Drottningholm. Bright Baroque blasts on the French horn. Pomp, the age of glory.

But it is in the Palace itself, in the gallery named after Charles X that I perhaps experience Drottningholm most profoundly. Bathed in light, you can look out over the Rococo landscape of the archipelago on the Mälaren side, while the terse Baroque austerity of the garden shines from the other direction, through the entrance hall with its staircase, designed by Tessin, filled with the sculptures of Antiquity.

Early one summer's morning, in July 1779, Bellman expressed someting of the same feeling as I am now experiencing, when he stood beneath Sophia Magdalena's window on her birthday, and sang:

> Drottningholm, thy splendour enchants,
> Everything in happy state.
> Sky is bright blue, high and clear,
> Billows glitter, wind rushes,
> Flowers blush, all fresh and cool.
> Trees full shadowy outstretching
> And with sprinkled leaves covering
> Cuckoos in the treetops sing.

Morning sun that nobly shimmers
Woods that glow from long way off
And on the water Amphion
With his golden lyre swims
Amongst the drumbeats, song and shots.
People's voices join together
And for Sophia Magdalena
Hearts beat tenderly and strong.

Gustav III's Consort died long ago and proud Amphion has made her final voyage, though the stern is still to be found in the Museum of Naval History. But the spirit of Bellman lives on in the park where "trees full shadowy outstretch".

My attachment to Drottningholm also derives from the fact that I lived for several happy years in the Wing of the Lord Chamberlain. A broad stone staircase rises between floors, and the drawing-rooms, which face the park, are filled with light from sunrise to sunset. Standing in the middle lounge is like being on the bridge of a ship, looking out over the sea of foliage created by the tops of the oak trees, with sunlight all around. "It is a friendly house, it has a friendly air", as Astrid Rudebäck used to say. She lived there before me. Lady-in-waiting to the late King. An energetic, gifted woman with a good sense of humour. I always felt I caught a glint of bygone times in her blue eyes, but more Rococo *joie de vivre* than chilly Gustavianism.

The Wing of the Lord Chamberlain has its own story. The first person to live there was Princess Sophia Albertina, sister of Gustav III. Her palace in Stockholm is also extant. "Sophia Albertina Aedificavit" is written in gold letters above the door of the Foreign Ministry on Gustav Adolfs Torg. Her lady-in-waiting was Magdalena Rudenschöld, mistress of the King's favourite, Gustaf Mauritz Armfelt. When the King died he was driven into exile by the new régime. Armfelt was accused of plotting to overthrow the Regency government and his downfall was also that of Magdalena who was condemned to death but pardoned. She was imprisoned under humiliating circumstances, pilloried before the whole people and drifted embittered and lonely out into the periphery of history. On an old manor in the distant wilds of Tiveden her diamond ring cut into a window-pane the following words: "O she who rested under the white shroud of nature".

I can see one particular scene in my mind's eye as I think of the old house. From the garden, in the Spring, you could see the bust of the Apollo Belvedere as it peeps out above the lilacs near one of the gables. The Classical god rises above a cascade of flowering lilac, blue as thunderclouds. Aphrodite was born out of the ocean foam near Cyprus. Could it be said that Classical culture was reborn in Sweden from the lilac blooms of Drottningholm? The image may be inaccurate as regards the history of art, but to me it has the right feel about it.

Then a car door slams shut, a window opens, music can be heard playing on the radio. I am back under the limes. But Drottningholm is not merely history. The Head of State still lives here, artists and writers continue to work, the Sweden of today continues to live and pulsate here in many different ways. There are perhaps many far more evident common denominators for Sweden, but as I sit on a noisy commuter train, rattling through sooty Bronx, Drottningholm is the heart of my Sweden. As I close my eyes, an image appears of the Palace in the light of morning and faintly, ever so faintly beyond the clatter of wheels, the music for Drottningholm by Johan Roman, floats forth under the limes.

Palace of Queens

The glittering waterfall of the cascades creates a white foam in the stone basins behind me. On the balustrade above, stand iron Baroque urns, green in colour, with the monogram of the Queen Dowager in gold: HERS, Hedvig Eleonora Regina Sueciae. A black and white wagtail flies jerkily over the bushy box trees of the parterre. The sweet, aromatic fragrance of these dark green shrubs in the warmth of summer.

There, in the distance, stands the Palace. Creamy yellow, stretched out, with a dark, copper roof shifting towards the green of verdigris. Above, the bright blue, enamel cupola of the sky. Perhaps the original colour scheme should have been retained: a rosy pink with grey windows and door frames. It is on the Castle in Upsala that these ancient colours of the Vasa dynasty remain. Such colours would have stood out pleasantly against the blue of the sky and the dull green of the foliage along the avenue of limes.

Within its golden circle, the clock on the façade measures out the hours through the ages. High in the sky, an aeroplane glitters silver as it descends towards Arlanda airport, and house-martins soar like stray notes up into the heavens above the Palace. They live under the eaves, further proof of the idyllic, rural quality of the place. They need mud to build their nests, grazing cattle to draw the insects, but also peace and quiet.

Drottningholm is not large by international standards. Not like Versailles or the Royal Palace in Stockholm with its six hundred rooms. Nor is it imposing or grand, full of the romantic notions associated with a castle on the Rhine, nor full of the weighty magnificence of a château in the Loire Valley, teeming with the darkness of the Middle Ages. Drottningholm can better be described as "lagom", that untranslatable Swedish word meaning approximately "suitable" or "just right". And here the notion is eminently suitable. A hybrid of pleasure palace and patrician villa from Roman times. No moat, no walls or battlements. Friendly, open and yet possessing stature. The austere Baroque façade softened by a touch of Rococo, invites the onlooker to share in its intimacies with an element of distance, but without being haughtily dismissive.

From the lake shore the Palace looks less formal. The perspective differs from that across the geometrical formality of the Baroque Garden. The picture is influenced by the water which is a living element and changes with the various nuances of daylight, and by the trees which break up the straight lines. A large willow down by the shores of the lake is said to have been planted by Queen Christina, one of the queens of Drottningholm. She abandoned the "true gospel" which her father, Gustavus II Adolphus had died for during one of the long religious wars of the 17th Century, and moved to Rome. One summer's day, nearly 350 years ago, she sailed out here. A willow twig had become caught at the stern of the boat. She planted it among some stones at the edge of the shore. A fairy-tale maybe, but one of the many details which give the Palace charm and personality.

When we look at Drottningholm from the lake shore we should not forget that that which now seems like the back in relation to the park and the Baroque Garden is, in fact, the main entrance. This is also the case with the Royal Palace in Stockholm, where the grand and dominating façade facing Helgeandsholmen and Gustav Adolfs Torg is, in fact, the rear of the building. The front faces the Old Town, which was, at the time, the centre of Stockholm. And out here it seems natural that the entrance is situated by the water, as it was by water that you used to arrive at Drottningholm. In "Suecia Antiqua" we see depicted a large and splendid harbour where Royal vessels could lie safely at anchor out of the reach of storms. It was never completed "because of the difficult and cruel shallows", but traces of the piles remain to this day. And other objects have also been found on the lake bottom near the Palace. Bottles, dishes, daggers and pitchers from the 16th and 17th Centuries, as well as clay pipes. Some of these have Gustav III's monogram. They were distributed for reasons of propaganda in support of the coup d'état of 1772.

Drottningholm is indeed a palace of queens. It started with Katarina Jagiellonica, the Polish princess who married Johan III. He was the

Finds made on the lake bottom, in front of the Palace.

Katarina Jagiellonica – the first Queen at Drottningholm.

son of Gustav Vasa, a ruthless, hard-handed Renaissance king who amassed power, absolute power, made Sweden into a hereditary kingdom, broke with Catholicism and confiscated the wealth of the Church. By his death in 1560 he had become the richest man in Sweden with five thousand manors and estates. One of these was the forerunner of Drottningholm, Torvesund Royal Estate, where Hans Dalkarl was Steward.

Traditions that vanish into the mists of time tell of royal connections with Drottningholm that are even older, though they are sometimes "of none too pleasant a kind". It is said that "King Östen was surprised at the castle which was then called Torvesund or Thoresund and was there burnt to death by the Jutish king whose name was Sölfvr, and whose rule over the Kingdom of Sweden was of equally short duration, as he was defeated and put to death by Östen's son, Yngvar Harra, father of the famous Braut Amund".

The historical realities behind these quotes are dubious, but raids and forays were among the grim realities of the time.

Johan III took over Torvesund from his brother, Eric XIV, whom he deposed and, it is said, poisoned. A brutal, but not uncommon, method during the Renaissance, where royal assassinations formed the red weft of the dark tapestry of history.

Yet King Johan was not only a man of *Realpolitik*. He also shared the appetite of the Renaissance princes for imposing architecture. "Building is our great joy" he wrote to one of his architects. Aesthetics and magnificence also had their political dimension. His kingdom "by the grace of God" was to be highlighted and accentuated in buildings. The enthusiasm of the Vasa dynasty for prudently keeping power within the confines of the family was not altogether shared by other powerful families.

In 1579, Johan III began to build a palace on the island of Lovön. He named it Drottningholm after his consort, Katarina Jagiellonica, daughter of King Sigismund (Zygmunt) of Poland and the Renaissance duchess of Milan, Bona Sforza. She was a fervent Catholic and came to Sweden with Catholic priests among her entourage and the guarantee of being able to freely practise her religion in that Protestant land. Royal marriages were in those days often the result of political deliberations. Eric XIV courted Elizabeth I of England in order to gain a powerful ally. As for Johan III and Katarina Jagiellonica, it seems, at least from a historical perspective, that feelings also came into play. When Johan, then duke, was imprisoned by his brother Eric in the castle at Gripsholm, Katarina accompanied her husband, sharing his captivity voluntarily. In her wedding ring is engraved the inscription, "Nemo nisi mors". Nothing short of death would part them.

Little is known about what the first palace at Drottningholm looked

23

like. It burnt down in 1661. It was designed by the leading architect of the Vasa era, Willem Boy, who, among other things, created Gustav Vasa's grand sepulchral monument in Upsala Cathedral. The palace was presumably a two-storey, brick building, with a score or so rooms on the ground floor. The upper storey consisted of a large hall and ten smaller rooms. There was also a chapel. A reredos in Botkyrka Church is believed to have originated there. From the shingle-covered roof a copper-plated tower rises, on it we can see a "gilded statue, flag in hand". To the North of the Palace, where the Chapel Royal now stands, there was a large wooden house with two floors for Court and servants. It was demolished during the 18th Century as it was considered to be a fire-risk.

Queen Katarina died as early as 1583. After her death, Johan III rarely made the journey out to Drottningholm. The last time was in August 1592. A description exists of how the King visited the deer gardens in order to see the fallow deer. The gardens lay where the park is situated today.

"Presently came the order that the lifeguards were to bring the forest creatures to the King where he stood with his men, who had previously been told to stand their hats here and there on the level ground so that the creatures, coming forth quickly and perceiving these hats, would become affrighted and alarmed. When the creatures were come and saw these hats they began to run hither and thither, up and down. This dance of the animals caused the King to become mighty glad and of good cheer and so beneficent that all those who had demands or complaints to submit to His Royal Majesty received favourable reply and leave."

But that very evening the King's health deteriorated rapidly and he died later that autumn.

The next in the line of queens at Drottningholm was the widow of Gustav Vasa, Katarina Stenbock. After her death in 1621, follow by a period during which the Palace had fallen into disrepair owing to ill-willed tenants, Queen Christina arrived on the scene, in 1649. She, in turn, presented the Palace to her mother, the Queen Dowager, Maria Eleonora, consort to Gustavus II Adolphus. At the beginning of the 1650s, the Palace became the property of the De la Gardie family. This can be seen as break in the line of queens, but this is not entirely the case. Magnus Gabriel De la Gardie's wife, Marie Euphrosyne, was, in fact, the sister of Charles X Gustav, successor to Queen Christina after her abdication. This was the beginning of one of the great periods in the history of Drottningholm. De la Gardie was Chancellor and one of the richest men in the kingdom, owning palaces and castles throughout the land. "He is the worst manager and the greatest wastrel in the world, has numerous servants, a grand table, and spends huge sums on household goods, the upkeep of the grounds and on building projects; it

Johan III, builder of the Palace, in the deer gardens where he became "mighty glad and of good cheer" when the fallow-deer "ran hither and thither, up and down".

is also said that he is building up forty or fifty estates. With such large expenditure he also needs a large income to help these enterprises along."

Magnus Gabriel De la Gardie, "quite assuredly the most handsome man in the world, with lively wit and natural eloquence", was a favourite of Queen Christina and took part in the Regency government formed to await the coming of age of Charles XI. But his lasting contributions have been in the field of culture. He brought with him many significant cultural impulses, not least by employing some of the leading artists and architects of the time, some of them from abroad.

De la Gardie restored the Palace at Drottningholm and made significant changes. Jean de la Vallée, the architect who completed Riddarhuset (The House of the Nobility), was put in charge of operations. But "princes are not to be trusted". Of this De la Gardie, who had influential rivals, was to receive concrete proof when the Palace was taken over by the Crown. The Crown had rewarded and compensated mainly the nobility with goods and land. This was felt to be unjust. "There are many lords and earls who have between sixty and seventy miles of estate as well as fine oak forests, and all of this has moved from the Crown into private hands, so that the King owns not so much as an oaken plank, having to pay for it if he wishes to acquire it." And the finances of the Crown were in a sorry state.

One more queen was to take over the first palace. Charles X's widow, Hedvig Eleonora of Holstein Gottorp, honoured the claim made on the Crown by De la Gardie, or rather by his wife, amounting to 30,000 Rixdollars in silver coinage. That was in 1661, the same year that the Palace burnt down, one cold December's night. The Queen Dowager had celebrated Christmas at Drottningholm, but had travelled back to Stockholm for the New Year. A few hours later, fire broke out at Drottningholm. "We had just spent eight days at Drånningholm with the Queen when the accident occurred; the same day we journeyed thence, the house burnt up four hours after we had departed. This was a great shame, but luckily the householdstuff was saved."

Hedvig Eleonora was the daughter of Frederick III of Holstein Gottorp. He was cousin to Gustavus II Adolphus and wanted to become independent of Denmark. Sweden could count on him as a loyal ally against the Danes. This was the calculation behind the marriage of convenience between Charles X and Hedvig Eleonora. But there were positive aspects, even at a personal level. "His Royal Majesty is happy and delighted at the arrival of the princess (she was eighteen years old at the time) and most pleased with her. In truth, she is indeed most beautiful and pious and has a promising aspect." In his letters the King called her "Mein liebes Herz", my dear heart. The marriage was to last but a few years. In 1660, the King died and "Her Royal Highness was much distressed in the presence of others and lies quietly abed".

Hedvig Eleonora, unlike Queen Christina and Lovisa Ulrica, was not an intellectual woman, and possessed "not a little harshness of character". She enjoyed good food and social life, especially card games. The Queen Dowager joined the Regency government for her son, Charles XI as well as her grandson, Charles XII, but she did not play a significant political rôle. She was interested primarily in the upbringing of her son, art and architecture. Nor did she lack the means. In jointure, the late husband's gift to his widow, she had received the counties of Gripsholm, Strömsholm and Eskilstuna. Later came the counties of Vadstena and Svartsjö. Hedvig Eleonora built both Strömsholm Castle and the Queens' Wing at Gripsholm in three storeys. She added two wings to Ulriksdal Palace and, after the fire at Drottningholm, she set Nicodemus Tessin the Elder the task of drawing up plans for a new palace on the site of the old one. "Das Haus kompt auf der vorigen Stelle zu stehen", as Tessin wrote.

Nicodemus Tessin the Elder was born in Stralsund in 1615 and was one of the key figures of Swedish architecture, being both city architect for Stockholm as well as Palace architect. He also sketched the plans for several towns in Norrland, among others Gävle, Hudiksvall and Härnösand. Tessin was also commissioned by Axel Oxenstierna. Kalmar Cathedral, in Italian Baroque, is one of his better known achievements. A trip abroad, during the middle of the 17th Century, to Germany, Italy, the Netherlands and France, had an important influence on his work which came to be shaped by French and Dutch traits. This is also evident in Drottningholm Palace.

In the spring of 1662, the year after the December fire, the plans were on the table and in April, Hedvig Eleonora laid the foundation stone "in the presence of several of the most important gentlemen in the land who laid under that very stone countless gold and silver coins, according to custom". By 1664, the shell of the main building was ready. Many took part. The work force consisted of nearly 400 men, carpenters, stonemasons, painters, bricklayers and many more. Soldiers were requisitioned. The Palace was not finished until after the death of Tessin. He died in 1681, but his son, Nicodemus Tessin the Younger, completed the work in about 1700. In the main, the exterior of the building looks much as it did then, though it was painted pink with grey window frames and door surrounds. The main building was connected to its four corner pavilions or wings by one storey instead of the present two. In the middle part of the Palace, there was also a high tower topped with a royal crown of huge dimensions. But the tower was too heavy and had to be removed.

By the 17th Century, Sweden had become a great power and a major force in the Baltic. The armies of Sweden swept victorious through the Germany and Poland of the Thirty Years' War. Large areas of

Denmark, Scania, Halland and Blekinge fell to Sweden, even if luck in war was not always the lot of the Swedish colours during the time Drottningholm Palace was being built. The building activities were not merely an expression of Hedvig Eleonora's personal ambitions and interests. They were also a manifestation of Sweden's rôle as a great power. But it is not unlikely that the level of ambition when building the Palace would have been lower if it had been built in the time of Charles XI. He was more a bureaucrat and an administrator than a spendthrift patron of palaces on a large scale. This is supported by a note made in the margins of history. The King had been given the option of buying a golden goblet. He had refused. The building at Drottningholm was swallowing all his money.

Drottningholm became Hedvig Eleonora's pleasure palace, a sunny idyll on the Mälaren, though she preferred Ulriksdal for practical reasons. It would take time before Drottningholm was ready. Her son, Charles XI, came here too, not least in order to hunt, as did Queen Christina. Of her the French Ambassador in Stockholm said: "I have seen her hunting in the saddle for ten hours at a stretch. There is no-one in Sweden more sure to stop a hare in full flight." And there was plenty of game, even wolf and bear. In later days, Charles XII would come here on hunting trips before proceeding eastwards on his Russian campaigns.

The Queen Dowager died in 1715, only a month before the arrival home of Charles XII from his many battles which were to prove the beginning of the end for the period of Swedish greatness. And when the King fell, at Fredrikshald, in 1718, Drottningholm went to another queen, his sister Ulrica Eleonora the Younger. She had been Regent at the death of Charles XII, but abdicated in favour of her husband, the hereditary prince, Frederick of Hessen who became Fredrik I of Sweden. He had, with success, taken part in the Wars of Spanish Succession under the leading generals of the time, the Duke of Marlborough and Prince Eugene of Savoy. His efforts as King of Sweden were less successful. He was unable to cope with the reaction against the Caroline autocracy. Both the Hats and the Caps, the two political parties at the time, were united on one issue: they had had enough of a strong and independent monarchy. Fredrik's political activity lessened and he devoted his energies elsewhere. "Love, the hunt and leisure occupied him all too much", and the fervently religious Ulrica Eleonora had to put up with the King's numerous escapades which were not always carried out with the greatest discretion. During her time, Drottningholm suffered a period of neglect in relation to the new Royal Palace in Stockholm, where building activities were all the time on the increase. Furthermore, Drottningholm was more or less finished by now. Ulrica Eleonora's efforts were concentrated mainly on décor and the interior of the building. She had the organ built in the Chapel Royal which was completed during her time. And she started the picture gallery in the Generals' Hall with its eighteen portraits of Charles XII's most illustrious generals, grouped around her belovèd brother, as well as a collection of those of her father, Charles XI's generals and leading collaborators.

Drottningholm's era of splendour began with another queen, Lovisa Ulrica. She was the sister of Frederick the Great of Prussia and was married to the Crown Prince, Adolf Fredrik, at a ceremony in Berlin in 1744, where the Crown Prince was represented by Carl Gustaf Tessin, patron of the arts, politician, cultural figure and son of Nicodemus Tessin the Younger who had succeeded his father as palace architect, also at Drottningholm. Carl Gustaf Tessin was to gain influence over the Royal Family, not least as governor of the future Gustav III, before he fell into disfavour and made his retreat.

All those making up the bridal legation were struck by Lovisa Ulrica's beauty and intelligence. "She is as fair as day itself." But in the background, Frederick the Great's discreet warnings against his sister's lust for power and capacity for intrigue could be heard.

She came to Sweden with a squadron of the fleet in the summer of 1744. Sweden was undergoing a period of change. The Caroline autocracy had gone to the grave with Charles XII, and the pendulum had swung in the other direction, so much so that her husband, Adolf

Ulrika Eleonora the Younger greatly, admired her brother Charles XII, was fervently religious and planned the interior of the Chapel Royal.

The era of splendour at Drottningholm began with Lovisa Ulrica, sister of Frederick the Great of Prussia. "She is as fair as day itself."

Fredrik, despite being King, found that his signature could be replaced by a stamp if he showed signs of intractability. But it was not only the political climate that changed, but the cultural climate, too. From the Baroque to the Rococo, from a deep belief in authority to the questioning cynicism of the Enlightenment.

On the 18th August 1744, the nuptials of Adolf Fredrik and Lovisa Ulrica were celebrated at Drottningholm Palace, which she received as a magnificent wedding present from Frederick I, who was also her godfather. "At this event, more splendour was displayed at the Swedish Court than at any time since that of Queen Christina." The King had held a reception down by the ferry at Tyska Botten, on the Bromma side of the water, where a Turkish tent had been pitched. And on Lovön, a distinguished retinue waited; the Crown Prince, the Council of State and the Court. Between the rows of lifeguards standing to attention, the parade approached the Palace. "Upon entrance to the Palace, Kettledrums and Trumpets could be heard", music which continued throughout the whole ceremony, and that evening "during the whole Banquet, a Concert was given by the Court Orchestra, which stood in the adjacent Reception Hall."

For these nuptials Johan Helmich Roman, "the father of Swedish music", had composed his splendid "Music for Drottningholm". It is from one of its movements that Bellman borrowed the theme of his ninth epistle, the one beginning "Dear brothers, sisters and friends".

Roman's music formed a symbolic vignette to the intellectual dimension that the young Crown Princess was to give the Court and the cultural life of Sweden. She had come from the brilliant Court of the great power of the time, Prussia, which was visited by such great men as Voltaire, to a Northern European outpost, at least from a cultural point of view. She arrogantly claimed of her father-in-law, King Fredrik, "He has a deaf conductor, a halt dancing master, a crippled fencer and a blind court painter".

A while ago, I was flying between two continents. Ten thousand metres up, high above Greenland glistening with snow, Roman's music could be heard via the earphones, vital, full of life, of joy. Yet when it was composed, Roman was a widower for the second time, a single father of five children and his hearing was gradually deteriorating. It is one of life's ironies that the "deaf conductor", as Lovisa Ulrica disdainfully called him, would live on many centuries after the nuptials at Drottningholm. While leading an obscure life, he conducted music that is now carried over a world where both Lovisa Ulrica and Adolf Fredrik have long been consigned to the annals of history.

Lovisa Ulrica's enlivening influence on Swedish cultural life found expression not least in the field of theatre. From Prussia she brought over a passionate interest in things theatrical and in her letters home she ridiculed the provincial actors of Bollhuset in Stockholm. She

29

engaged a troupe of French players and built a theatre at Drottning-holm, in 1754. When this burnt down eight years later, she replaced it with the present theatre. Leading Swedish architects were given the task of rebuilding her palace. "Drottningholm is a delightful place", she wrote. "It will give me pleasure to beautify it and make a number of alterations." To the connecting wings and corner pavilions a storey was added, and she built the lakeside wings on the southern side of the Palace, as well as the buildings in the Canton part of the grounds. For the brothers and sisters of the Crown Prince she built a hunting lodge and a Chapel Royal, both of these wings between the Palace and the Court Theatre on the northern side. As a birthday present, one fine summer's day, she received the Chinese Pavilion, which Adolf Fredrik had had built in great secrecy. When damp and rot destroyed it, she built another Chinese Pavilion, shining through the foliage on Flora Rise.

Lovisa Ulrica also collected works by Chardin and Boucher, leading artists of the time. Many objects came from the collections of Carl Gustaf Tessin, which he had been forced to sell for economic reasons.

If Lovisa Ulrica showed an interest for international art, she was much less tolerant of things Swedish. She cleared out a great deal from the former art collections at Drottningholm in favour of work mainly by the pastel painter, Gustaf Lundberg.

But her interests spread beyond art and the theatre. Carl von Linné (Linnaeus) was in charge of her natural history collections. Gyllen-borg, Creutz and other writers belonged to her circle, and in 1753 she founded the Academy of Learning, which held its first meeting at Drottningholm. They strove for "pure taste, a tidy mind and a digni-fied style of writing"

Perhaps her contributions to the arts were somewhat overshadowed by the brilliance of her son, Gustav III, the "Charmer King". Person-ally, I have a suspicion that Lovisa Ulrica was more seriously interested in the various expressions of culture than her aestheticising son. Not least the collection of manuscripts and her large library gave proof of her many-sidedness and depth of knowledge. For Gustav III art and literature were not merely ends in themselves. They could be subordinated to greater schemes, i.e. his political aims.

Lovisa Ulrica's political life was not as successful. She had no sympathy for the reactions of the Age of Liberty with its antipathy towards autocracy. Her ideal was the "enlightened despotism" of Prussia, and she openly opposed any limitations placed on royal power by the Royal Council. It went as far as an unsuccessful coup d'état in 1756, when eight persons who supported the Royal Couple, with Count Brahe at their head, were executed for their complicity.

There was also friction between mother and son. The political marriage of Gustav III and the Danish princess, Sophia Magdalena,

Canton viewed from the rise where Castor and Pollux stand.

proved impossible for Lovisa Ulrica to accept. Nor did she ever fully accept her daughter-in-law. The marriage throws light on the marriages of the time. Carl Gustaf Tessin and other leading politicians forced the marriage through to create more friendly relations with Denmark, which had always been a doubtful piece in the game of Nordic power politics. The alliance contributed to the fact that Tessin fell from favour and left his post as Governor to the Crown Prince as well as from other high positions.

Politically, Gustav III succeeded better than his parents. In 1771, the year after acceding the throne, he made a bloodless coup which greatly strengthened the power of the King. But it widened the cleft between him and Lovisa Ulrica, whom he had hoped would take over her share of the increased functions of the King. The break became a fact at the birth of the Crown Prince, the future Gustav IV Adolf, in 1778. The rumour spread that Gustav III was not the father of the child and the Queen encouraged it. Lovisa Ulrica disinherited her son and wrote in her testament: "If you, under whatsoever pretext, shrink back to the slightest extent, then tremble, for I shall utter the curse which all ungrateful sons deserve." The suspicion was not lessened by the fact that Lovisa Ulrica was forced to leave her beloved Drottningholm for economic reasons. The Palace was sold to the Crown and was taken over by Gustav III, with the right of disposition.

At Drottningholm there exists a portrait of Lovisa Ulrica at that time. It shows an agèd, care-worn and bitter woman. In a diary it said of her that "in her later days, her complexion was ruined, her teeth marred, her breath strong, but her mouth was pretty, her laughter pleasant, her nose small and well-proportioned, whilst always being stuck up in the air".

From Drottningholm, the Queen Dowager moved to Fredrikshov, which lay in the vicinity of Oscar's Church, in Stockholm. One wing remains intact today.

The next Queen at the Palace was the Danish princess, Sophia Magdalena. Her life was not a happy one. One son died as a child, her husband, Gustav III, was murdered, and her son, Gustav IV Adolf, was deposed and exiled with the revolution of 1809. Later, she was to experience the humiliation of welcoming to Sweden the new Crown Prince, Marshal Bernadotte. She was despised by her mother-in-law, Lovisa Ulrica, and Gustav III treated her with a mixture of tolerance and chill. Much has been written about her difficult situation, which was not made any easier by Gustav III's sexual ambivalence. "It could not be concealed that he found no pleasure in making offerings to the Goddess of Love", as someone commented. And her royal sister-in-law, Hedvig Charlotte, wrote: "Never did she become capable of overcoming a great shyness, a result of her strict upbringning. Her father, King Frederick V of Denmark, had treated his daughter with nigh on harshness."

Sophia Magdalena's first visit to Drottningholm and her meeting with the Swedish Court after the journey from Denmark is well-documented. In a letter from the young Ebba Bonde, we read: "My Lord, how beautiful she is, was on everyone's lips. For myself, I cannot say I found her beautiful, though I later found her most comely. This was hardly surprising under the circumstances, as she was weary after the journey, had run a temperature throughout the morning and had been occupied with her toilet, and what was worst of all, was greatly in fear of the Queen." Her fears were well grounded. Lovisa Ulrica's jealousy combined with her aversion for Denmark and all things Danish, as well as her fear of losing her influence over Gustav III, not least now that his royal offices had been extended, turned her into a formidable opponent for a shy, frightened twenty-year-old girl far away from her family and country.

Gustav had fallen between the Devil and the deep blue sea, an understanding for Sophia Magdalena's difficult position and a fear of outbursts of hate from his jealous mother, who "loves you madly". The

Carl Linnaeus put in order Lovisa Ulrica's collection of naturalia. About Linnaeus she wrote: "He is very interesting and clever, but one has to overlook the fact that he is a little boorish."

Crown Prince's former governor, Fredrik Sparre, wrote that Gustav: "exhibits a sickly, servile, falsehood brought forth by the terrible Lovisa Ulrica". And from the festivities at Drottningholm when Sophia Magdalena came to Sweden, Axel von Fersen wrote: "The Crown Prince showed great indifference towards the young princess and neglected so patently all those attentions concomitant with her position, rank and beauty, that the whole court began to wonder and grew indignant".

The Crown Prince himself wrote about his relationship with Sophia Magdalena: "Unless one is a Prometheus and can steal a spark of holy fire, it is impossible to breathe life into that statue..."

The King's favourite, Armfelt, sums up her situation: "His young, neglected consort he treated with coolness, and that belovèd Princess, who bore alone the burden of Royal brilliance, was one of the least happy ladies in Sweden."

With such an active and domineering man as Gustav III there was little scope for Sophia Magdalena to set her seal on Drottningholm. She was often there, the summer visits by the court were often extended into November, but she also visited other pleasure palaces such as Karlberg, Ulriksdal and Gripsholm. Gustav III devoted all the more interest on the palace. He extended and expanded. The Dukes' Stables, the House of the Escort, the Pharmacy and Treasury buildings all rose on Malmen, where plots were let out for handicraft and trade. Bridges connecting with the mainland were built and the Marshal of the Court's Wing and the Queen's Pavilion were begun between the Court Theatre and the Palace proper, forming counterweights to the other wings. The King let Desprez plan the Theatre foyer and the Breakfast Lounge, and he built the Gothic Tower, Vilan and the Governor's Residence in the park. An English Park with antique statues was laid out and Gustav III changed some of the interior of the Palace, at times in a manner at which art historians of today raise an eyebrow.

But it was not merely architectonically that Gustav III influenced the development of Drottningholm. The King was also an ambassador of French culture, introducing to Sweden the international currents of the time. He transplanted them into a square-shouldered Swedish idyll where the sunny glittering of Lake Mälaren replaced the turquoise Mediterranean and where junipers were reflected in the ponds instead of cypresses. Perhaps his contribution can be compared with the building of the Royal Palace in Stockholm. This too brought to Sweden architectural influences, interior design, sculpture and painting from abroad. Also out at Drottningholm, during the long summer's days, art, opera and the theatre would flourish and further cultural development with consequences which would be felt throughout the land. The creation of a palace of the intellect, if you will.

And now the shadow of politics was to fall across the stage of reality where Gustav III occasionally could not withstand the temptation to act theatrically. He played for high stakes at great risk, declared war on Russia, tried to break the power of the gentry and extend his offices. Disaffection spread. Against all advice he had instituted a monopoly on the manufacture and sale of spirits. "Complaints, grumbling, curses and threats were heard in the capital and in all the provinces of the realm." In Stockholm, the poverty in some of the poorer districts was terrible. Out of every one thousand live births, 430 died. A report from 1772 states: "The distress exceeded any suffering that a human being could imagine, the houses were filled in the main with the most serious of diseases. People lacked clothing, and there was not the slightest piece of food to fill one's belly with."

It was against such a background of suffering that the grand spectacles out at Drottningholm were played. Opposition to the King grew and culminated in an assassin's bullet at the Stockholm Opera on the 16th March 1792, the year before Louis XVI and Marie Antoinette died on the guillotine in Paris. The King was attending a masked ball when the shot was fired. A tragic but appropriate end for a theatrical King.

The shot at the Opera ended a cultural renaissance inspired by the King. Drottningholm was also adversely affected. Gustav IV Adolf visited the Palace but sporadically, while Sofia Eleonora preferred the more modest Ulriksdal. One of the few occasions on which the Palace blossomed forth, was in 1797, when the King came there with Frederika of Baden, his sixteen-year-old consort, before their ceremonious procession into Stockholm. The festivities continued for eight days and among those attending was Märta Reenstierna, the lady from Årsta who, in her diary, tells of "the glittering vanity of the arrival of the Royal Couple". It was at Drottningholm that Gustav IV Adolf organised the last carrousel in 1800, which took place in the grounds of the Palace.

Though he was to see it one more time in 1809. After the coup d'état, when disaffection against him had been turned into action, he was transferred to Drottningholm where he was kept under arrest for eleven days in the Chinese Lounge, guarded by no less than five hundred men. The sad journey continued by sledge over the ice to Gripsholm Castle and out of Sweden. Much later he would die, unhappy and alone at the "White Horse Inn" in St. Gallen, Switzerland as Colonel Gustavsson. March is a fateful month for rulers. Gustav III was shot on the 16th, Gustav IV Adolf deposed on the 13th, and Brutus murdered Caesar on the 15th, the Ides of March.

Duke Karl, the brother of Gustav III, became Charles XIII in the autumn of his life. His Consort, the quick-eyed and gifted Hedvig Charlotte, has meant a great deal for our knowledge of Drottningholm, not least by cause of her indiscreet diary entries, but as Queen she did

34

The Theatre Museum in the Queen's Pavilion.

not influence the development of the palace very much. Nor did her marriage prove a happy one. Charles XIII did not, in keeping with the custom of the day, restrain himself too much in his relations with women, within or without court circles. He also became more and more senile. Wicked tongues had it that he now and again became involved in "one or two for his age most violent skirmishes under the banner of the goddess, Venus".

Charles XIV Johan, the French marshal, who brought the Bernadotte dynasty to the throne of Sweden, showed little interest in Drottningholm. This also applied to his consort, Désirée. Her enthusiasm for the snowy country near the North Pole was very circumscribed. Apart from a shorter visit from December 1810 to June 1811 it would take twelve years before she came to Sweden to stay.

The Palace fell gradually into disrepair, the collections were dispersed. The death of Gustav III had already brought with it a reaction against the King which was to have dire consequences for Drottning-holm. The collections were taken over by the State, the portraits of Gustav III and Sophia Magdalena were hung away in the attic of the Palace and in 1793 one hundred and twenty-four paintings were sent to Gripsholm. At the beginning of the 19th Century the natural history and botanical collections were transferred to the University of Upsala and the Academy of Sciences.

It would take until 1846 in the main before the Sleeping Beauty slumber of the Palace was broken by a prince in the shape of Oscar I. Using mostly their own means, he and Queen Joséphine began to restore the Palace, an enterprise that was continued by his son Oscar II. With Gustav V and Queen Viktoria of Baden the 20th Century saw a large amount of restoration activity, both as regards the Palace and the grounds. The Queen was especially interested in the park and she "joined the ranks of those queens who had lavished much love and thought on those splendid grounds".

With interest, love and skill, Gustav VI Adolf continued the restoration work, not least on the Chinese Pavilion and the park and grounds. The Palace was, for a time, home for him and Queen Louise. But it was Lovisa Ulrica who was the last queen to set her personal seal on Drottningholm by way of building projects. After her and Gustav III's era, the Palace became more of a family home than a "palace of queens". Other pleasure palaces came into the picture such as Ulriksdal, Tullgarn, Sofiero and Solliden, to name but a few.

And now the wheel has turned full circle and once again the Palace is home for a young family. A new link has been forged on the long chain of queens. To names such as Hedvig Eleonora, Lovisa Ulrica and Viktoria, Silvia has been added. But many of the two hundred rooms are still open to all who wish to step into a piece of living history, where the Palace of Queens reflects that which was and echoes past occurrences.

The shot at the Opera put an end to Gustav III's cultural renaissance.

"Nowhere Can You Find a More Beautiful Theatre"

Flames rose up against the dark night sky, a crackling shower of sparks floated down over the marsh where the alders grew behind the Court Theatre. The Chamberlain, Riddarstolpe, squeezed his way past the mass of panic-stricken people, carrying little Princess Sophia Albertina in his arms. "The whole building was now in flames and burnt like a torch."

It was a late summer's evening in 1762, the 25th August, Lovisa Ulrica's namesday. An opera was being performed at her new theatre. The Royal Couple was there with the whole court. "Each and every one of the members of the audience admired the play and the room was so full of gentlemen and ladies wearing hoop petticoats that people were almost on top of one another." But suddenly, after the fourth act, one of the singers "Comédienne Madame Baptiste" came running right through the theatre. Everyone thought this belonged to the play, but the lines she was repeating could not be found in the manuscript. Fire had broken out "caused by the negligence of a boy who had been careless with fire in the vicinity of a vessel containing turpentine".

The theatre fire was not the first at Drottningholm. As early as 1753 we hear of "the old playhouse", which is believed to have stood near Muncken Rise at the far end of the French Baroque Garden. And in the Palace itself, in the Hall of State, amateur performances were given which also occurred at other palaces and castles where the young successors to the throne lived. They were often demanding plays, written by authors such as Voltaire, Corneille and Racine, played of course in the original language, the French of Court and nobility. And it was from Court circles that actors were recruited. Lovisa Ulrica writes on this subject after her wedding. "Soon, I shall be able to enjoy both tragedy and comedy, played by persons of high station who have come together to entertain us."

Ever since she arrived in Sweden, Lovisa Ulrica had wanted to engage a troupe of French players. Her great interest in the theatre which had been awoken at the court of Frederick the Great at Potsdam, could not, in the long run, be satisfied by amateurs from among the nobility. And the professional performances at Bollhuset in Stockholm, which lay in the vicinity, caused her to write home to Berlin in terms which made it clear that she turned her nose up at them. The reviews were far from flattering. But it was not until she became Queen that she was able to realise her plans. A troupe of French players was, as such, no innovation in Sweden. Charles XII, more known for warfare than culture, had, as far back as 1699, invited Sieur de Rosidor and his ensemble to Stockholm. It was Nicodemus Tessin the Younger that lay behind these plans and his instructions to the diplomat Cronström in Paris, were very precise. The troupe had to be equally versed in comedy as tragedy, it had to be capable of music and dance and it was not to be forgotten that the actresses had to be pretty. This proved to be the beginning of a wide range of cultural initiatives as regards French drama which were to be continued by Lovisa Ulrica and her amateurs. But they did not play only in French. Olof von Dalin, one of Gustav III's tutors during his time as Crown Prince, and a leading author, wrote a play which was performed in Swedish in the Palace grounds in 1752. This was the first time that Swedish theatre had been performed in these circles during the 18th Century, and the cast list with such actors as Bielke, Falkenberg, von Düben and Strömfelt had in it a number of important Court names. But von Dalin would come to grief after the unsuccessful coup d'état of 1756. He was accused of having made "injurious" allusions about the Four Estates in the play.

Lovisa Ulrica's French players came to Drottningholm in 1753. First they played at the Confidence, the former horse-breakers' residence at Ulriksdal Palace, which the Queen had Adelcrantz turn into a theatre. A year later, the Queen began to build a new theatre which went up in flames only a few years later. It was not only plays that were performed here. There was also opera. An Italian operatic group under the

direction of the conductor, Uttini, had been engaged, and royal occasions were celebrated with his works such as La Galatea, L'Adriano and Il Re Pastore. Mozart too, as well as other 18th Century composers, was played here, especially Gluck, the leading light in the heavens of Gustavian opera, with works such as "Orpheus & Eurydice". The theatre repertoire included Molière, Corneille, Diderot, Voltaire and other "great" names. Much of this repertoire is still performed at Drottningholm.

Then came the fire of 1762. This did not however, smother Lovisa Ulrica's interest in theatre and opera. As Carl Gustav Tessin wrote in his diary, a few days after the fire: "There is already talk of a new theatre built of stone." The Chief Steward, Carl Fredrik Adelcrantz, who was able to "supervise all that belongs to the theatre and festivities at the Court" was put in charge. His post was the equivalent of the present day Director General of the Ministry of Works, whose previous title was approximately Chief Steward. The task was to prove to be a dubious honour which brought disaster to his economy. Adelcrantz paid a good deal of the building costs out of his own pocket, but was never reimbursed. He was obliged to sell his house in Stockholm and mortgage his manor at Trångsund. When he had paid the interest on the loan to build the theatre, 150 Rixdollars remained of his salary to live on for the rest of the year.

By 1766, Adelcrantz' work was finished, its austere façade having risen on the spot where the old theatre had stood. Like a phoenix from the ashes, though the new Theatre was twice the size of the old one. A young gentleman of the Court, a certain Claes Julius Ekeblad, writes about the unofficial opening ceremony in his diary:

"The new playhouse is now ready, and Their Royal Highnesses have gone thither to inspect the décorations. All the candles in the auditorium have been lit to give an impression of what it could look like. Nowhere can you find a more beautiful theatre, and I must do Adelcrantz the honour of mentioning that it is a masterpiece. The Queen requested the Crown Prince to declaim something, which he also did."

He recited a tirade from "Iphigénie et Tauride". Princess Sophia Albertina then played a scene from "Le Philosophe Marié", and finally, Miss Brita Horn, who had the most beautiful voice in the world, sang a delightful aria from "Le Roi et le Fermier". "Their Royal Highnesses returned hereafter to the Chinese Pavilion."

I agree with Ekeblad. And a latterday observer, the world-renowned architect Le Corbusier, agreed with him. Nowhere can you find a more beautiful theatre. I am not so much thinking of the austere Classicism of the exterior, but of the interior, the auditorium and the stage. In an ingenious way, Adelcrantz fused the two parts into a spacious and pleasing whole and created the illusion of both reality and unreality. Stage and auditorium are not divided into two halves, different in nature with the curtain as a dividing line, they are the mirror image of one another. Originally candles, and now specially manufactured electric bulbs, have the same warm yellow flickering effect. When the gorgeous curtain rises, two worlds, the brightly lit stage, and the dark, passive auditorium do not in fact form separate entities. Instead, they merge together into a whole, and the gentle, living light giving new dimensions and shades of light to the scenery and costumes, which would be lost on a modern stage. A pulsating, living blend which is accentuated by the architecture and the sets. Adding to the illusion of the 18th Century, is a wealth of detail in the costume and orchestral instruments, the players in their white Rococo wigs. Furthest forward in the auditorium stand the two gilded Gustavian armchairs, one for the King, one for the Queen, also hard benches covered in blue cloth, copied from the original upholstery, with their place markers from the time of Gustav III. Behind the Royal Couple and entourage sat, for example, "unpresented Ladies and Women of the Burghers", and furthest back, lower functionaries such as "the Man and Maidservants

The "old" operas are still performed with the original scenery.

The wind-machine at the Court Theatre

and Coiffeurs of the Princely Court".

But it was not only Adelcrantz whose economy was bad. Lovisa Ulrica could not afford to continue to live at Drottningholm when she became a widow in 1771. The running of the Court became too expensive and in 1777 she sold the Palace to the State handing over Drottningholm to Gustav III. Such an autocratic king as Gustav III made little distinction between grant of enjoyment and rights of ownership, and he made use of the Palace as if it were his property. A new period of greatness began at Drottningholm, and not only there. His era set a trend and he gave his name to a period of art history, the Gustavian period, which was a high point never to be repeated in the history of Sweden. Art, architecture, interior design. Names such as Haupt, Sergel, Roslin and Adelcrantz. But aesthetic considerations were not the only ones determining the actions of the King. Gustav III was a calculating politician determined to get results and he also used art to further his aims. As early as 1771, when he ascended the throne, he had new ideas for the theatre. For Lovisa Ulrica and her circle the theatre had been a natural source of entertainment and amusement at a brilliant court. But Gustav III also used the theatre politically. He wished to create a national, Swedish theatre which in the tradition of European cultural heritage stood on its own two feet. A theatre where plays were performed in Swedish, not French, to reach the people and to unify the country round national, historical events. When he, as Crown Prince, visited Paris in 1771, he was informed that Adolf Fredrik had passed away, and by the 3rd March he had already written to Stockholm ordering the dismissal of the French troupe of players. In this matter too, poor Adelcrantz became the scapegoat for the Royal lack of financial responsibility. He was obliged to pay the salaries and travel costs of the players who were still sending in claims to Stockholm at the beginning of the 19th Century. And they could hardly be accused of indolence during their sojourn in Sweden. Over three hundred and fifty plays could be found on their repertoire during the twenty years they stayed there.

After the French troupe had left for home, Petter Stenborg and his troupe entered the stage. Stenborg also ran "Rotundan", a popular summer theatre in Humlegården, a park in central Stockholm, where the statue of Linnaeus now stands. A popular tradition of comedy arose here which, by way of August Blanche and so-called "bush theatre", led to the revues of the 20th Century. One of the actors remains today in Operakällaren, but this is not the cellar to the Opera House, but a restaurant. A type of brandy is named after Carl Stenborg, the actor. It is called "stenborgare", i.e. Stenborger, and is flavoured with Seville oranges, fennel, aniseed and sugar. It should be held for a moment or two in the mouth between inflated cheeks, then swallowed rapidly, all in the manner of Stenborg. A herb-flavoured "källarskorpa", another

43

delicacy, should be eaten along with the "stenborgare".

The audiences cheered the performances of Stenborg's troupe, but the connoisseurs pulled a wry face. After the première, Ehrenswärd, who was to become the director of the Stockholm Opera, wrote: "I cannot satisfactorily describe how I was plagued. One's hearing was tormented at every word, the manner of the players was tasteless and it was with not a little sad astonishment that one beheld this spectacle."

But the King had hit the mark. Theatre in Swedish was what the people wanted. Ehrenswärd continues: "... I have never seen such a large number of people, applauding at every word and seeming to possess an inner joy at seeing a Swedish spectacle, and it seemed that the public in so doing were appealing to His Royal Highness to patronise such art."

In his diaries there are entries on "the rise of the Swedish théâtre", and Ehrensvärd assures us that "every word in this documentary shall be true". He points out that "without King Gustav's taste, insight and encouragement, the Swedish théâtre would never have been altered, transformed and improved in such a short time, this enterprise having become dear to the general publick and admired by all foreigners".

Gustav III was a realist. He did not begin to make his influence felt in Swedish drama but went the long way round via opera, Swedish opera. There were excellent artists to be had, both singers, dancers and musicians. By way of music, song and dance, Swedish drama could be smuggled onto the audience among the opera scenery. "One hereby grows accustomed to the language, its harshness is reduced by captivating music." The King was very much involved, also as an author. Among other things, he wrote the libretto to the opera, "Gustav Wasa" in 1786, which is one of the highlights of Gustavian opera and one of the greatest Swedish operatic successes of all time. But it should not be forgotten that the King was assisted in his literary efforts by such authors as Kellgren who elaborated on his various ideas, sometimes with "repeated groans". Erik Gustav Geijer writes how he was taken by "Gustav Wasa" at the Stockholm Opera, during his youth. The Desprez settings contributed to its success. During his journey to Italy, Gustav III had been impressed by Desprez both as an artist and as an architect, had put him in charge of the Opera staging and taken him on as an architect. In this way he came to influence the development of the theatre at Drottningholm, both through his dramatic scenery and outside by designing the Breakfast Lounge which he planned on the suggestion of Gustav III.

The King wrote other librettos such as "Christina" and "Birger Jarl" in order to make Swedish history live for the people. He was also interested in the audience reaction to the use of the Swedish language: "The King has consulted all countesses and ladies on whether they were offended at the use of their mother-tongue when it was spoken so

The "stenborgare" – an aquavite flavoured with Seville oranges, fennel, aniseed and sugar – lives on at the restaurant Operakällaren as a greeting from the actor of the Gustavian era, Carl Stenborg. A herb-flavoured "källarskorpa" is to be eaten along with the "stenborgare".

nakèdly, without music. All curtsied and declared themselves for the language of the country. The wife of Countess von Fersen was the only one who did not feel comfortable with the expression: darling, but when the King later repeated this to the Director of the Academy of Learning, the Right Honourable Count Carl Fr. Scheffer, the latter replied with his usual vivacity: Oh! Your Majesty need not ask Countess Axel Fersen's opinion, for she has throughout her life heard naught but: Amant! Amant!"

Gustav III also encouraged all who contributed to his efforts to make Swedish the language of the stage. Judge Sotberg, who had translated a play into Swedish receives "a diamond ring to the value of 200 ducats; and among the eminent people who played, the King has distributed gold boxes, gold watches, stuffs, fans etc.".

In 1781, the King engaged a French troupe under the leadership of the famous Boutet de Monvel from the Comédie Française, not least in order to instruct a new generation of Swedish actors. At the première, Monvel played "with such verve and inspiration that after the play was over he had to be carried from the theatre in a faint". Boutet de Monvel was a pioneer of the stage in that he spoke instead of declaiming.

ustav III on his way to the fateful asquerade at the Opera.

The King liked to act and much was written in contemporary diaries and letters about his interest in the theatre and his activities as an author, director, rehearser and actor. Even if we have to remember that these comments were written by people who were very critical of the King, there are many insights into the odd make-up and complicated nature of his personality. The whole of his childhood was characterised by imagination and make-believe in the atmosphere of intrigue around Lovisa Ulrica and Adolf Fredrik, where every word was noted and weighed up, every utterance was interpreted, a milieu where gesture spoke louder than words. Walls had ears and the attempted coup by the Royal Couple in 1756 failed with punishment and executions in its wake, all this when the King was but ten years of age. Gustav III himself carried out two bloodless "revolutions" during his reign, before he himself fell victim of the ultimate conspiracy, the one that ended his life. His childhood, combined with a disjointed and whimsical upbringing, coloured by his mother's changes in mood, was to mould his personality. "There is not one honest hair on his head" wrote one commentator. Another commented: "He was weak and unmanly, exaggeratedly vain..., skillful, fickle, cunning and talented as regards dissembling, and sought constantly to achieve his aims by thousands of devious ways. He loved pomp and circumstance and always put make-believe before reality."

And what was the pompous ceremonial of the Court if not theatre? In this artificial hothouse environment, Gustav's interest in the theatre was inflamed into a passion. When he was seven years of age, a member of the Court wrote: "The Prince's devotion to spectacle became a passion. He never went to bed before the small hours. His governer at the time, Count Scheffer – who had succeeded Tessin – trying to find the cause thereof himself, saw the Prince drag a table to his bedside, climb up onto it, and, after having declaimed scenes from tragedies for a couple of hours, gave himself a feigned stab of a dagger as he cast himself into bed, falling asleep immediately." Scheffer himself wrote how, long after he should have been asleep, the Prince would stand on his bed and declaim to himself. "Theatre makes such a deep impression on him that only one performance suffices, especially if it be a tragedy, to be held fast in his memory. It is especially noteworthy that ladies' rôles are most rapid affixed there, and among these, the rôles of those who were most beautifully dressed."

In contrast to the usual picture of aesthetic tendency we get of Gustav III, we have the opinion of his sister-in-law, the clear-sighted and observant Duchess of Södermanland, Hedvig Elisabeth Charlotte. In her diary she mentioned, having dealt with the King's effeminate tastes, not least in jewellery, his "dreadful slovenliness, which also causes his teeth to be dirty and ugly and his breath foul-smelling. Despite his interest for finery and glittering costumes, he dresses carelessly, and it happens on occasions that his kneebreeches are so ill-fitting that his bare knee sticks out".

As King, Gustav III played his rôles, not only in real life but also on stage. At Christmas 1775 and the New Year 1776, to name but one example, twelve plays were performed in a fortnight with Gustav III in eight of the leading rôles. He often came from a performance in costume to dine at Court when he was not eating with the actors. "We have thus seen him as Rhadamiste, Cinna and as the High Priest of the Temple at Jerusalem, causing himself to become the object of ridicule at his own table".

Other commentators were more positive. "That evening there was another performance of Cinna... Mistress Caroline Lewenhaupt performed a miracle in her rôle as the countess in the second play 'The Wager', so that the French Ambassador declared that one could not see better at any theatre in Paris. The King was very good as the colonel. On Wednesday, January 10th, the tragedy 'Cinna' was performed again as a titbit and it went even better than before. As follow-up we had 'The Englishman at Bordeaux'. The King played marvellously."

But criticism was growing. The French Ambassador, d'Usson, called to the King's attention how it was "unworthy for the King to deck himself in the attire of a player". This caused Gustav III, despite his passion for the theatre, to withdraw from the stage, at least as an actor.

The King soon found that the old stage at Bollhuset was not suffi-

*The revolving stage was operated by six
young men.*

cient for "National Theatricals". The theatre was, moreover, a fire-risk. As early as 1773, he had bought the palace from the De La Gardies on what is now Gustav Adolfs Torg in Stockholm, to make out of it a theatre, and he himself drew up plans which were, in the main, carried out. The task was given to Adelcrantz and in December 1774, he produced a well thought out plan for a building with an almost identical façade to that of Sophia Albertina's palace opposite, nowadays the Ministry of Foreign Affairs. The King approved the following year and by 1782 the Opera was ready. It was opened the 30th September, "in the presence of their Royal Highnesses with the opera 'Cora and Alonzo'. The higher civil officers of the Realm, the Foreign Minister, the Colleges and Estates as well as the Burghers of Stockholm were invited to this occasion. The excellent taste of song as well as of the action with which this Pièce was played, complemented by a large and well conducted orchestra, of richesse of dress and splendour of Décoration, which were interspersed with earthquakes, volcanoes, e.t.c., all carried out with order and quickness; in a word, the noble and beautiful fusion which was everywhere present, gave proof of the heights of perfection which our National Théâtre has reached. It must also be mentioned in favour of the Swedish Genius and Wit that this opinion was not only borne by those unprejudiced foreigners as were present, but also by the more enlightened parties among our fellow countrymen who, with respect to this Spectacle said that rarely had they seen anything of equal brilliance and perfection."

When the Opera was scandalously demolished in 1892 and afterwards rebuilt, the poet Oscar Levertin wrote: "When I look at the different-sized lumps of stone that have replaced Gustav III's beautiful Opera... I get the impression that Stockholm has suddenly been conquered by strange barbarians."

Bollhuset was also used after the opening of the new Opera. It was given over to Monvel's French troupe in 1783 and the King had quite advanced plans to build a theatre for the Royal Swedish Dramatic Theatre, which also played at Bollhuset. One curious note in the margins of history is that Ristell, who was also the librarian at Drottningholm, pawned valuable items in the coin and medal collections to save the theatre from bankruptcy. He did not succeed and fled to Paris.

Gustav III was to come to mean a great deal not least for the Court Theatre at Drottningholm. Actors and other personnel were invited out to the Palace when the King was in residence and were allowed to stay in the theatre building itself. There were detailed instructions to be followed. The conductor, Uttini, and the ballet-master, Gallodier, were to receive two bottles of wine a day while the rest of the troupe had to satisfy themselves with less. "All dancers and lady-dancers receive one bottle of wine each and figurants a half, figurantes a third of a bottle and even children receive wine."

The actors' rooms are still furnished with the original furniture and hand-painted wallpaper. The wallpaper alone is unique and is one of the cultural and historical rarities at Drottningholm. The theatre has a larger collection of 18th Century wallpapers than is to be found in the rest of Sweden. During the summer months Adelcrantz lived here as well as, occasionally, Baron Armfelt when he was director of "His Majesty's Spectacles". He shared the King's interest in Swedish theatre. "I shall attempt to show at the Royal Theatre to what extent it is possible to express oneself with gentleness, with feeling and naturally, in the Swedish language", he wrote to Princess Sophia Albertina.

Gustav III's weakness for theatrical effects was also evident outside the walls of the theatre. There are many charming examples, for instance before his journey to Italy in the autumn of 1783. The King had suggested to the Queen and his entourage that they should take an evening walk through the park. At the gates stood a guitarist who sang humorous songs, and further along the avenue a soothsayer told the fortunes of the royal ladies and praised the Queen. The ballet from the Opera danced contredanses in an arbour and a little comedy was performed using the clipped hedges of the open-air theatre as a back-

Gustav III's troupe of French players was led by the famous actor Boutet de Monvel of the Comédie Française. He played the première "with such verve and inspiration" that he passed out.

drop. In the other avenue stood a market with lanterns in the trees and stalls with "galanterie", coffee, wines and spirits. The Court was kept entertained by the Court Orchestra and the evening ended with a supper at the Chinese Pavilion.

The King's interest in opera and theatre was also expressed in large and well-rehearsed carrousels which he arranged in the grounds of Drottningholm. Here too, he combined business with pleasure. The King talked about the necessity of having a noble soul housed in a strong body and wrote that the tournaments "entertain among the nobility the heroic soul, the righteous demand for honour which is necessary for an estate intended for the defence of the realm; they set barriers against the feebleness which, along with the customs of recent times, has crept in unannounced and which weakens, the body entirely depriving the soul of all energy and strength". In the grounds the Galtarean heights were taken by the gentlemen of the Court in opera costumes and they fought against fire-breathing dragons and they whirled about in "the Magic Wood" dressed up as Greeks, Romans, Chinamen and Indians. In the grounds we can still find the space where carrousels took place, on the northern side, beyond the ponds, as a reminder of Gustav III's interest in the Middle Ages. The times were full of chivalrous ideals and in Paris splendid tournaments and carrousels were being organised. The areas to the south of the Palace, near Flora Rise were also put to use. Castles of painted linen and other scenery were erected against the background formed by the rise. Stands with canopies were built for spectators, fire-breathing dragons appeared and pistol shooting competitions on horseback were run, as well as fencing and attacking "Turk's heads" and "quintans", i.e. dummies, on horseback, with a lance. Hillerström has in his great tableaux described the battles of the knights with dragons and evil spirits.

We can get some charming insights into the activities at Drottningholm. It is Magdalena Rudenschöld, lady-in-waiting to Sophia Albertina, who tells the story. Her unhappy love-affair with Gustav Mauritz Armfelt was to lead to dishonour and humiliation but this she did not as yet know when she wrote:

"The King came back from Italy in August 1784 accompanied by Baron Armfelt. All who have seen and known this man will agree with me that he epitomises all that could capture even the most fickle of women's hearts. I saw realised in him the beautiful ideal of my dreams for which I had long sought. For a moment he seemed to wish to mark me out from all the ladies of the Court to whom he to a greater or lesser extent paid court. To be able to capture the most handsome and belovèd of gentlemen of the Court was something that flattered my vanity ... At that time, Armfelt in no way occupied himself with things of state, he arranged festivities for the Court and paid homage to

Gustav III had a passionate interest in the theatre, wrote plays, directed and acted. He also used the theatre for political ends. By staging plays in Swedish, he wanted to rally the nation around national, historical events.

beauty wherever he found it. His interest in me was but fleeting, but the impression it made continued to lie in my heart and only my pride allowed me to conceal this fact and seem indifferent when he entered into the conjugal state with Countess De La Gardie, who now is his wife... The King, who had much encouraged this liaison, was overjoyed that it had come about and celebrated their wedding with a number of festive occasions. The whole Court who at that time were at Drottningholm, rehearsed a magnificient carousel which was to be a re-enactment of the Fall of Jerusalem, after Tasso. The most pretty and young ladies of the Court were to take part in this occasion. The countesses Höpken and Löwenhjelm, known for their grace and loveliness portrayed the tutelar goddesses of the Mussulman host and guided the king, who was their knight. He portrayed Rinaldo from whom I had removed the spell of Armida. I rode on a fine white horse and was clad as a nymph with bare neck and arms, with a belt glittering with diamonds and a white veil which fell down over my horse like a fluttering piece of drapery. Accompanied by Rinaldo, I rode forth at a gallop and brought him to the judges of battle. My entrance made a great impression on all the spectators: I received applause from every quarter and people assured me that I was as beautiful as ever. That which convinced me most of all of this was the impression I made on Baron Armfelt, which did not escape my attention. I enjoyed this triumph exceedingly."

The interior of a box

A little about Armfelt, the favourite of Gustav III who perhaps was closest to him. Gifted but superficial, spiritual and elegant, a realist bordering on being a cynic. An exponent of the Gustavian Court, as we like to imagine it to have been, but in this Armfelt was the exception rather than the rule. The King appointed him Lieutenant-General, Governer-in-Chief, Chancellor of the University, Director of the Opera and Member of the Swedish Academy before he reached thirty-five. And these are but a few of his distinctions. The writer Jan Olof Olsson, known as Jolo, has summed him up in one sentence. "One of the Gustavian men-of-the-world and men-about-court, traveller, womaniser, diplomat, soldier, poet, cultural figure: it seemed quite natural for him to take part in a battle, storm a Russian position, seduce a lady of the Court, write a little poem, conclude a treaty with a foreign power, write the repertoire for an opera house or write a contract with a publican." A glowing meteor in the 18th Century sky. But the glow faded after the death of Gustav III. Armfelt fell victim of the new régime and was condemned to death for "treason against King and Realm, was deprived of his noble status and knightly privileges, also of his honour and glory. And shall, like... forfeit his life and be beheaded..." But he was pardoned, and in due course came to serve under Gustav IV Adolf, was involved in the revolution against him, became a citizen of Russia in the pay of Tsar Alexander and took part

The actors' stairs

in the war against Napoleon. The fate of a man.

And at the theatre performance followed performance. Artists such as Elisabet Olin, Carl Stenborg and Jacques Marie Boutet de Monvel appeared on the 19-metre deep stage where even Bellman gave guest recitals. Down in the trap-room and up in the flies a labyrinth of pullies, ropes and ingenious wooden constructions were responsible for gods floating down from the rosy heavens and for the change of scenery from Hades to the Elysian Fields. Waves could roll in the background and a large stone ball in a wooden trunk deriving its origin from Elizabethan theatre gave the frightening illusion of thunder. The machines which were constructed by Donato Stopani is unique. It is still in working order today and is the only machinery of its time that has been preserved.

51

The Theatre too remains intact, as it was built by Lovisa Ulrica and Adelcrantz, with the exception of the New Lounge or Breakfast Lounge, an addition to the West side of the building which Gustav III had built following the plans of Desprez from the beginning of the 1790's. The name stems from the fact that the Court used it as a breakfast room, the meal eaten to the accompaniment of music from the gallery.

Gustav III died on the 29th March 1792, murdered by a pistol shot during a masked ball on the 16th at the Stockholm Opera, an assassination which inspired Verdi to write the opera "Un ballo in maschera" (The Masked Ball). There is something deeply symbolic in the way he died. Gustav III was christened in the main hall of the Wrangel Palace, a hall usually used for theatrical performances, but which had been cleared for the christening. As Crown Prince he had opened the Court Theatre at Drottningholm before the official opening by reciting from the stage and word reached him that he had become King by way of the Countess of Egmont in his box at the Paris Opéra. He meant more for Swedish culture, theatre and opera than any other Swedish king and was shot by an assassin at his Opera, wearing fancy dress. He loved to act, and both in public and private life hid himself behind masks.

Silence fell over the theatre at Drottningholm when the echo of the shot died away. But not quite. Gustav IV Adolf, the King's son, arranged a carrousel in the grounds as late as 1800 and on several occasions during the 1850's scenes were staged of, among other things, "Maria Stuart" by Schiller. Though the war against Russia, the dethronement of Gustav IV Adolf and the events surrounding the latest successor to the throne, Napoleon's marshal, Jean Baptiste Bernadotte, brought a harsher reality and realism than jousting and operatics. The theatre was overshadowed in its overgrown parklands, dust fell over the stage. The chords of the cembalo died away among burnt-down candles and no god descended from the flies down onto the stage. The dull rumble of thunder ceased.

One of the few occasions on which the Theatre was used during the 19th Century was when Gustav V was born in the Queen's Pavilion, one of the yellow wings between the Theatre and the Palace, the one nearest the Baroque Garden. It was in 1858 when a group field artists of the time, a troupe of French zouaves on their way home from the Crimean War, gave a performance of "101 coups de canon", one hundred and one cannon shots. The reason was the birth of the Duke of Värmland. In the play, a group of French tourists met a number of Dalecarlians and they discussed as to who was the greatest, Gustav Vasa or his comtemporary, the French King Henry. Suddenly shot of cannon were heard. The Frenchmen, thinking war has broken out, cry "Aux armes", but are reassured by the Dalecarlians who succeed in

The Court Theatre Orchestra in 18th Century costume.

dampening the fiery Latin temper and tell in a leisurely manner that a prince has been born. They embrace to the tones of the Marseillaise. Could this be heard from the pavilion where the Prince in question, grandson of one of Napoleon's marshals lay sleeping? Perhaps his grandmother was in the audience at the theatre: Queen Désirée, erstwhile fiancée of Napoleon? It would not be the first time she heard the song of the French Revolution, though it would be the first time it had been heard on stage at Drottningholm where revolutionary strains were not exactly encouraged.

Now began the long period of hibernation for the theatre of Lovisa Ulrica and Gustav III. Parts of it were used as a store, granary, stonemason's workshop and in Desprez' Breakfast Lounge prayer meetings were sometimes held. But the myth of the "deus ex machina", the god who descends from Mount Olympus and puts everything right, lived on in the old building. One day in the late winter of 1921, chance, or "Fate" to use the language of the theatre at Drottningholm, would have it that the art historian, later professor, Arne Beijer came here. His special field was Gustavian theatre and he came with a couple of the staff from the National Museum, to look at objects stored by the museum in the theatre building. Beijer wanted to see a painting by Hillerström which portrayed Gustav III's tournament in the park at Drottningholm.

To reach the storeroom it was necessary to cross the old stage. "Time and time again, we bumped into large wooden frames and weirdly carved profiles in the dark." The frames consisted of the old scenery and Beijer had, by accident, stumbled upon a goldmine as regards research into Gustavian staging. And so the Theatre was awakened out of its long slumber. The machinery, still intact from the 18th Century, was put in working order again. Lights were installed, the decorations restored and both the stage and auditorium were restored to their former glory.

The première of the "new" Theatre took place on the 19th August 1922, the 150th anniversary of Gustav III's coup d'état. On the programme were arias by Gluck and Rococo dances performed by a ballet ensemble. From that day on, the Theatre has been in operation and every summer operas and ballet performances are given stemming from the 18th Century, often from the original repertoire including such names at Mozart, Händel, Haydn and Gluck, to name but a few. Ballets such as "Cupid Bound" are danced out on the sloping stage. There are also performances of dramas, a recent example being Molière's "Don Juan". And the performances are still announced by small pages in white Rococo wigs and 18th Century costume, ringing silver bells.

The Theatre at Drottningholm is unique as it is the only 18th Century stage with complete scenery, machinery and décor; even if other theatres such as the one at Gripsholm are equally well preserved. It does not, of course, play the leading rôle it once did in introducing European culture to the country behind the pine curtain, but it opens a door to a living past. A museum which at the same time functions as a living institution, where the association "The Friends of the Theatre at Drottningholm" makes a significant contribution. Though there is a "real" museum in the Queen's Pavilion, where Gustav V was born. There are kept unique collections of theatrical historical interest such as sketches for scenery, paintings, engravings and much else that throws light upon Baroque and Rococo theatre. They come, for the most part, from Tessin's collections. There are, for example, woodcuts from the 16th Century from the *Commedia dell'arte* tradition which are unique and form the oldest documents of their kind. Nicodemus Tessin the Elder made many important purchases, but it was his son, Carl Gustav Tessin, who was responsible for the majority of the acquisitions. At auctions, he acquired lots of objects from Prince de Carignan, the Director of the Paris Opera.

I have often stood, of an evening, in the park by the Theatre. Have seen the pale yellow, almost white building with its roof, black as soot, against the unreal pallor of the summer sky where the light has stood still between dusk and dawn. I have seen the gentle glow from the windows, heard the distant 18th Century music from inside, listened to the cascades of sound emanating from the old instruments. The ponds in the English Park glitter against the night sky. A door opens, a man in a Rococo wig and white knee-stockings matching his silk clothing walks slowly under the trees. One of the singers out for a breath of air, or someone else, someone completely different?

The Chinese Pavilion in the Park

The heavily laden rafts glide slowly over the smooth water. It is an early summer's morning in July 1753. The sun is rising, bird song floats on the air over Lovön beyond, and there is no time to lose. There was a bustle of activity at the arsenal in Stockholm to get Count Gustaf Tessin's order ready on time. And he was not just anybody. His grandfather and father had planned and built the Palace at Drottningholm. Now the Count had decided, purely for pleasure, to erect a small Chinese pleasure palace in the style of the time, out at his castle on Åkerö island. Time and again, he came in haste and with impatience to inspect and urge on. For everything had to be done in a hurry when the order came from high up. Swearing and sweating, the men had loaded the sections onto open-sided wagons which had clattered down to the quay and the rafts.

But it was not to Åkerö that they were going, and it was not Tessin who had ordered it. It was the King himself, Adolf Fredrik, and the Chinese Pavilion was secretly smuggled ashore onto Lovön in jointed sections. The sections were mounted on a rise in the grounds out of sight of the Palace. With the same cloak of secrecy, the furniture had been ordered in the name of various Court officials, and the plans had been drawn by the King himself, even though Hårleman and Cronstedt had, in fact, held the pen. Secrecy was important, for the pavilion was to be a surprise, a birthday present for Queen Lovisa Ulrica on the 24th July, the same day as she held the inaugural meeting of the Academy of Learning that she had newly founded.

The Queen's Birthday was celebrated with theatre, but not in the "Old Playhouse", but in the Hall of State at the Palace. The Playhouse was situated on Muncken Rise, and a performance there would have revealed the King's plans. After the performance, the carriages were given the order to make a tour of the grounds. The equipage stayed furthest back and the Queen wrote in a letter that the King drove her "down by the pleasure gardens, and I was surprised to be standing before a veritable fairy-tale, for the King had built a Chinese pavilion, as beautiful as can be. The Cadet Corps were dressed as if they were guards to the Emperor of China, and two of the King's aides-de-camp were in command, wearing the uniforms of military Mandarins. They carried out Chinese exercises. My eldest son stood by the entrance to the pavilion, dressed as a Chinese prince with the gentlemen of the Court in attendance, dressed as civil Mandarins. He read out a poem in my honour, thereafter handing over the keys of the pavilion".

Enthusiasm for the Chinese ceremonial was not as great among all participants. The cadet, Adlerfelt, who took part, told of how he thought it "absolutely ridiculous" to exercise in Chinese. On the great day, the cadets got up at two in the morning in order to be exercised for three hours from five o'clock onwards by the King himself. They then marched up to the Pavilion. "There we were met by Lieutenant Duwall again and both we twenty-four cadets and our officers were put through the ridiculous Chinese exercises for the last time... As soon as this was over, we all dressed up as Chinese and shortly after came twelve members of the Court Orchestra, also these in Chinese dress and we then practised these idiocies for more than an hour."

Adlerfelt also describes what happened when the Queen opened her presents which "cost the King three tuns of gold".

"At six o'clock the King and Queen came driving up attended by a great suite, all in closed carriages. We stood with our musick without the gates of the Chinese Pavilion. Our two cannons we had with us... The Crown Prince came out of the Main Pavilion, followed by the whole of his retinue, carrying a red velvet cushion with gold keys lain upon it. The cushion had gold tassels and a broad fringe, and the keys were three in number. He went up to the Queen as soon as she had passed through the gate and presented the keys, saying a few words in Chinese, which he himself did perhaps not understand. At first she did not recognise him, but then she gave him a kiss, accepted the keys and he followed with his suite right up to the Main Pavilion...

When the Queen had seen and praised everything and told the King

58

of her gratitude and delight, everyone went into the spacious hall of the main pavilion and coffee and other refreshments were served to those exalted persons and their suites."

But, as Adlerfelt bitterly complained, the cadets were given nothing to eat. Though they made up for it later that evening. "That evening they feasted and drank so much that they could not retire and were obliged, much to the King's displeasure, to lie in the open air."

There followed a theatrical performance with a backdrop by Johan Pasch, "a masterpiece, fifty-two ells in length and thirty-six ells high". It portrayed a waterfall between high mountains. The two operas lasted until two o'clock in the morning, involving fifty actors and three hundred extras. The supper and ball lasted until six o'clock. The festivities continued for eight days.

It is not hard to imagine the scene that took place over two hundred years ago. The King, happy with the enthusiasm of anticipation at the Queen's reaction. Her astonishment on seeing the small palace that had grown out of the greenery from one day to the next. The Chinese music, the Mandarins and the Imperial Guard. And then she discovers her own son, as excited as a seven-year old at the prospect of presenting his Royal mother with the gold keys on a velvet cushion. The evening sun on the park and the excitement of the cadets of being able to come so close to their King and Queen. A Rococo idyll, an idyll of a royal family. And I can remember the bright spring evening much later when a young queen stands on the steps outside the Chinese Pavilion full of anticipation as she welcomes her consort to a surprise dinner on his birthday.

How did it come about that Adolf Fredrik built a pleasure palace in the grounds of Drottningholm? A contributory factor was that everything Chinese was then in vogue. There were two discoveries made during the 18th Century that were to be of significance for the history of art. The first was China, the second, Italy, or more precisely, the excavations at Pompeii and Herculaneum. The Chinese influence left its mark on the development of the Rococo, while the austere architecture of the Romans was highly significant for the Gustavian style.

Interest in China and Chinese art was great all over Europe. The Queen's brother, Frederick the Great, had built a Chinese pavilion at Rheinsberg, only a few years before, and there was a large collection of Chinese porcelain at Drottningholm. Hedvig Eleonora had already collected a great deal of porcelain, material and other things from China and Japan. In the Queen's "Prayer Room" alone could be found 151 items of porcelain. They were displayed according to the fashion of the time, on open stoves and in niches. Her successor, Ulrica Eleonora the Younger, also collected porcelain. Inventories show that from the 1730s onwards, she had hundred of pieces of porcelain at Drottningholm, forming one of the largest collections of Chinese porcelain in

Some details from the Chinese Pavilion.
Top, a negro with lion in terracotta. Above, a jolly fat Chinaman in
porcelain. The little carriage in lacquer and gilt stands in the Ante-
Room of the Cabinet, where the wallpaper with the blue birds is to be
found. Furthest right, a corner of the Green Lounge.

Sweden. This is to be seen against the background of the fact that the East India Company, which imported large amounts of porcelain, was founded in 1731.

Many factors lay at the root of this interest in China. A good deal of missionary work had been undertaken, particularly by Jesuits, and trade was rapidly expanding. Travelogues were published, the earliest of which included descriptions such as those made by Marco Polo, and the Rococo was empassioned with exoticism and refinement. The earliest mark of Chinese influence was in ceramics. Right up to the 17th Century, Europe had not learnt how to manufacture porcelain, and the potteries of Delft imitated Chinese patterns on faience, especially in blue and white. During the 18th Century, the patterns were also used at the porcelain potteries of Sèvres and Meissen as well as Nymphenburg, to name but a few. Another field was that of interior design and furniture manufacture, and the books of designs produced by the Englishman, Chippendale, who had been influenced by Chinese stylistic ideals, were, in their turn, most influential. It was from China that he took the strong, straight chair legs and lacquered furniture. Another area of design where chinoiserie blossomed was that of wall-decorations, panelling and wallpaper, where Watteau, among others, was a seminal figure in bringing China to Europe.

When Lovisa Ulrica stood in front of her little pavilion more than two hundred years ago, she saw before her a red-painted, single storey building on a grey base. The window frames were green and at the corners stood trunks of palm in silver and green. The roof was of sheet-metal, but over this a yellow tent with dragon ornamentation was spanned, with bells, large and small. At the centre of the building stood a large hall, connected on either side with a smaller room. There was also a room in each of the wings. Elsewhere in the Queen's letters to her mother we read that: "the interior is proof of the generosity and of good taste of the person who designed it, a beautiful hall, decorated in the finest Indian (chinese) style with four vases of porcelain, one in each corner. In the adjoining rooms there were old Japanese lacquered cabinets alongside which there stood sofas upholstered in Indian materials, all this in the best of taste; there was a bedroom decorated in Indian material and a bed of that same material and also the walls were adorned with the most beautiful types of porcelain, pagoderie, vases and birds."

The little pleasure pavilion did not only have an aesthetic function. Here, it was possible to "return to nature" in the spirit of Rousseau, somewhat similar to that which Marie Antoinette tried to achieve at Trianon – the ethos that made shepherdesses out of ladies of the Rococo Court and that peopled the glades with fauns. It became an exclusive "retraite", away from a hectic official life filled with, among others, the demands of protocol. Lovisa Ulrica's Chinese Pavilion and

62

The Chinese Pavilion and the Confidence

Peter the Great's "Mon plaisir" were both expressions of the same need.

"In this Chinese Pavilion, a rare phenomenon in our chilly North, the Royal Couple, Adolf Fredrik and Lovisa Ulrica, spent their most pleasant and carefree hours, resting from the trying cares of government and the oft-burdensome weight of the Royal Purple. Here they were boundlessly happy, and stayed on well into the autumn. Here the King cut in wood and was fully the mild and friendly soul. Here the proud Queen was most woman, here her overweening genius did not burn like a blinding flash of lightning, it merely shone as mild as the Nordic summer sun, here she babbled with her children, joked with her own sex, was satisfied with life around her and its cheerful conversations, and often occupied herself with spinning and sewing."

Other descriptions stress the importance of both the Chinese Pavilion and Drottningholm itself as sanctuaries, but seen from a different angle: "It was thus here, in the lap of art and nature, that the high-minded but restless Queen, who bore the celebrated name Lovisa Ulrica, sought refuge from the stormy seas of politics. Here, Frederick the Great's proud sister could forget the humiliation of bearing a crown without power... here, the murmur of the embittered strife of the parties did not pursue her, here both Caps and Hats, the two political factions were condemned. Thwarted in her plans to put a more powerful sceptre in the hand of her weak but kind-hearted consort, she fled here to the greening isle, and the hurts she bore in her breast felt less bitter."

I always stop when I enter the avenue that comes down from the park. I know that the Pavilion is there, I know what it looks like, but every time, for some strange reason, is the first. In pink and yellow under a roof of green cooper, a little Rococo pavilion lies with its touch of China, built on a mound of stones and moraine against a background of spruce and pine soughing solemnly under a heaven of Swedish blue. A crow flaps clumsily over the roof. Dragons and Chinese heads watch me expectantly. An equally unlikely meeting as stumbling upon a Rococo shepherdess wearing a broad-brimmed hat, white skirts and a periwig, carrying a crook, on a woodland path. The Palace itself, down by the lakeside, lies securely and consciously anchored in its own being. It has grown from century to century, while this Chinese pleasure palace, on a rise, is like a treasure lost by a careless giant on the run from a completely different world. "A fairyland" as Lovisa Ulrica wrote. Though perhaps, it comes into its own in the late autumn and winter when the leaves have fallen and the branches of the tall trees frame the façade in black and grey, with the naked branches forming graphic strokes of Indian ink against a grey sky.

For me, the Chinese Pavilion epitomises the idea of the Rococo. The style had changed from the pompous and ceremonial formality of the Baroque. Changed from posturing narcissism to lightness, movement and intimacy. The parquet flooring shines, the polished furniture shimmers, silks glisten. A sensual affirmation of life. Flashes of light in a waterfall of glass prism, Mother of Pearl and lacquer. Light falls through the high, French windows. On pastel coloured walls hang paintings with motifs from "la fête galante", the happy, aristocratic pastoral idyll, signed with such names as Watteau, Boucher and Fragonard. The Chinese Pavilion epitomises the expression "l'art pour l'art" – art for art's sake.

Going in through the doors is like entering into a jewel case. I know of no other building, no other rooms that have awoken in me such an intense aesthetic experience and joy, other than the rooms forming the

The long wall of the Blue Lounge

interior of the Chinese Pavilion. In a limited space, we can find the best of Swedish Rococo in concentrated form, colour and design. The interior is also unique in the fact that most of its contents are original. When Lovisa Ulrica was obliged to leave Drottningholm, in 1777, a thorough inventory was made, including a list of contents of the Chinese Pavilion. We therefore know that around 75 % of the original furniture remains. The rest consisted of pieces of furniture such as small tables and chairs. An even higher proportion of the Chinese and Japanese collections has been kept.

But it is to be remembered that it is not the original Chinese Pavilion that we are entering. There, fires could not be lit. Nor was the quality of workmanship particularly high, as the building was constructed in "ready to assemble" sections. Damp and rot spread through the Pavilion. "As fungus took the upper hand and ate away at the Pavilion, Their Majesties decided, in 1763, to let it be built anew of stone..."

The Pavilion was demolished, and Adelcrantz, Treasurer of the Court and architect of the Court Theatre at Drottningholm, was given the task of drawing up plans for the present Chinese Pavilion, the construction of which was completed in 1769. The whole of the Royal Family took an interest in the Pavilion and when the foundation stone had been laid, on the 2nd June 1763, the brickwork was pointed by each member of the family in turn using a silver trowel, as well as by both the Treasurers, Adelcrantz and Cronstedt. The builders received extra rations, and the master builder was presented with the trowel.

The first room you enter is the Marble Hall. It is more traditional, of European style. The chinoiserie is that of the Chippendale chairs and the gilded lead reliefs, on the walls. Straight ahead lies the Mirror Room, this too decorated in the traditional manner, mainly in French Rococo, but with a touch of the Gustavian, especially in the walls. There is also a screen, that Princess Sophia Albertina embroidered for her brother, Gustav III, in the form of a hanging Chinese basket of flowers. To the right, lies the Queen's workroom with panelling on the walls, in gold and red, surrounding wall-coverings in white silk with Chinese-inspired embroidery. According to tradition, Lovisa Ulrica and her ladies-in-waiting embroidered them and thus the room is called the Embroidered Room. The large porcelain figures around the walls once belonged to Hedvig Eleonora, while the potpourri jars in blue and white were the property of Queen Christina.

The Bedchamber, to the left of the Mirror Room, is decorated in green, mauve and silver. Here stand a pair of lacquered Japanese cabinets and Chinese paintings in Gustavian frames, but these were brought to the Chinese Pavilion a little over a century ago. It is not strictly correct to call the room a bedchamber. There was only a sofa for the Queen to rest on and strangely enough, no-one actually slept in the Chinese Pavilion apart from Oscar I in connection with a military

Oriental porcelain cock

66

exercise. More "Chinese" are the Yellow and Red Rooms which flank the Mirror Room. The panelling is in bright yellow and red with black Chinese lacquered screens fixed to the walls. In the Yellow Room, the screens depict the city of Canton. The décor is, in the main, by Jean Eric Rehn who followed the foremost authority of his time, William Chambers, who was born in Gothenburg but worked in London. His work, "Designs of Chinese Buildings, Furnitures etc." which the author sent to the Royal Couple, was seminal in the transformation of the Chinese influence into practical décor.

Through the West Gallery, we find the most beautiful room of all, the Blue Lounge. The floor is pale yellow, the wall-panelling bright blue with gold surrounds and the decorated tapestries have "Rococo-Chinese" motifs after Watteau and Boucher. A Chinese screen in black and gold. Black Rococo chairs with red saffian leather cushions against the blue of the walls, and in the corner, magnificent potpourri jars in *famille rose*. The Green Salon, in the eastern half of the Pavilion, has a more markèdly Chinese profile than the Blue Lounge. Here too, Boucher has been the inspiration for the chinoiserie of the woven wall-coverings.

A narrow, steep flight of stairs leads from the Marble Hall to the floor above. Here lies the cosiest part of the Pavilion. The height of the ceiling is lower than that of the reception rooms, and the walls are not panelled, but covered in wallpaper or silk with Chinese bird or flowers, both in pastel and on stronger shades.

Chinese mandarin

Up here, we find the Octagonal Room with its framed drawings in Indian ink by Lovisa Ulrica and Gustav III as a child. Romantic landscapes with ruins and rocks. And here lies Gustav III's workroom with its Chinese mirror paintings, Chippendale chairs and the King's private writing desk. If one stands in the middle of the Oval Room, the acoustics prevent one from hearing what is being whispered by people standing or sitting around the walls. They can, on the other hand, hear one another. This was perhaps practical in times when Court intrigue was rife.

In the Library, Chinese and Japanese figures have been placed on consoles in the same way as in the days of Lovisa Ulrica. And we know the arrangements to be true to those of her time, as the figures have made shadows on the original wall-coverings, which have become faded by the light. Many of the books on the shelves have stood there right from the start, marked "bibliotheket på China". Geography, science, history and other subjects, including "shameful illnesses", are represented in the finely bound volumes with a small Royal crest on the cover and a sheaf, symbol of the Vasa dynasty, on the spine.

The Chinese Pavilion was not used to spend the night at. When the day was over, occasionally after the sun had come up, the guests returned to the Palace proper. But the needs of mortals were, nevertheless, catered for. Behind a door covered with wall-paper, in the Ante-Room to the Cabinet, stands a splendid Gustavian armchair which has been converted into a "night stool".

The Pavilion also has two detached wings. Moving West to East, we have the Silver Chamber and the Billiard Room. Lower, nearer the park, lies the Confidence. The Royal Family used it as a dining-room when they wanted to eat in peace, out of the earshot of attendants and servants. The Confidence is ingeniously constructed so that the dining table can be laid while it is standing at ground floor level and then raised into position. The same goes for the circular dumb waiters with their shelves for the various courses.

In the eastern wing beyond Flora Rise, lies Adolf Fredrik's Pavilion with its Turnery and Carpentry Workshop. It has been discussed as to how much he actually practised turning. But all are in agreement that he died of a surfeit of "*hetvägg*", a mess of bread and milk, eaten one Shrove Tuesday. Though it was not only the "*hetvägg*" that was to blame. Johan Gabriel Oxenstierna writes that "the King died of *hetvägg*, sauerkraut, meat and turnips, lobster, caviar, red herring and Champagne. This is not the most dignified way of dying, it is the death of a parson".

The Sentry Tent a little further away in the park, is newer. It was erected by Gustav III after plans drawn by Adelrcrantz. In design, it is nearest to a Roman legionary tent, but it also resembles a copper engraving from "Chine Illustrata", resembling a Chinese military encampment.

But the light, relaxed and familiar atmosphere during the time of Lovisa Ulrica and Adolf Fredrik was to change. For the Pavilion, where the gifted and strong-willed Queen and her less decisive Consort relaxed with their children and their hobbies, far away from the eagle-eyed politicians who replaced the King's signature with a stamp, underwent a change involving the close adherence to a schedule drawn up by Gustav III. At a quarter to two, a procession was made by carriage from the Palace to the Chinese Pavilion. At two o'clock, dinner was served in the Blue Lounge and at the Confidence. During the afternoon, books were read in the Library, the guests played billiards or cards and at seven o'clock, the carriages started out on a *promenade*. At ten o'clock, supper was served, and at midnight, the whole company drove back to Drottningholm. There were also other stipulations. So that the Court might know as to whether or not the King was to spend the day at the Chinese Pavilion, a playing card was affixed to the door of the Ante-Room at the Palace. The King of Hearts denoted the Chinese Pavilion, the King of Spades, Drottningholm. The sister-in-law to the King, Hedvig Charlotte, comments a little bitterly: "It happens, occasionally, that the card is changed twice or thrice during the course of one day, causing much inconvenience." This is

The Chinese Pavilion is, for me, the epitome of the Rococo.

understandable, not least as the King required different dress for each of the venues. The hectic Court programme should also be seen against the background of the King's pronouncement that "There is nothing worse than boredom for a thinking being".

Armfelt, the King's favourite, though also observant and free from illusions, wrote about the Courtly life of Gustav III: "Without taking into account the resources of the land, he wished to have a court similar to that of Louis XIV, hold banquets and envelop himself in the same splendour as the French King. The old aristocracy, which had been crushed under Charles XI, was once again raised to a position of importance; it was called a treasure of the Realm and treated with great reverence. Every artist, every learnèd person of note, was sure to enjoy not only the patronage of Gustav III, but also his favour and friendship."

In a letter to Princess Sophia Albertina, Armfelt wrote, at the beginning of 1788: "On Tuesday, we had a masked ball, today, Friday, another; every day a spectacle takes place, often two different ones. One would like to imagine that people are enjoying themselves, but I fear that an evil spirit holds sway, as everyone looks as if he were at a funeral. In a word, here is the reason: the participants consist, in part, of those who have much to do, in part, of those who have nothing to do, but would like to; finally, there are those who neither have, nor wish to have, anything to do. For the first-mentioned, the revelry is only a form of relaxation after a hard day's work; the next type do not enjoy themselves because they take exception to everything, criticise everything, find fault with everything they themselves did not think of; the third type yawn, sleep, eat, demand nothing and enjoy nothing."

There are many descriptions of life at the Court of Gustav III containing contemporary memoirs and diaries. One such entry gives us a description of the King's "*lever*".

"Nearly every morning at ten o'clock, the King received visitors. A number of generals and officers of all ranks, civil-servants of higher station and landed gentry assembled in a room without the Great Bedchamber and waited there until the King had had his hair done and was dressed up to the waist. The doors were opened as His Majesty put on his shirt, an operation which occured with much panache, without disturbing his coiffure. The King sported a noble but

Masquerades were a popular feature at Court.

70

affected air; the bushy, but much powdered hair contrasted with his face which was of a deep scarlet hue. The gentlemen of Realm and Court, who had taken up their positions in the entry hall stood in a half-circle behind the King, while those entering completed the circle and stood in nervous anticipation of a glance or a word from the King. When waistcoat, tailcoat and medals had been put in place with great skill and alacrity before a mirror, the King came forth. Those who were unknown to the King or had been absent for some while were now presented. Those who belonged to the Court or to leading regiments or to the Crown Prince's own regiment or were themselves of a certain rank, had the dubious honour, which our present King has never wished to bestow unto his subjects and which the majority of Courts in Europe have now dispensed with, of kissing the hand of a man. When the presentations had been made, the King went round the circle. His observant eye had already made note of whom it consisted. And he weighed up in his breast how many words he ought to devote to each and every one. The least honour was a gracious nod, thereafter came an "How do you do?", whereafter a short conversation, while the greatest honour was a longer conversation. This joy was not merely in the flattery of gracious attention. He spoke so quick and clever that it was a joy to hear. Happy was he who could but answer somewhat that occasioned an "ha-ha". This would prolong the conversation. The King's laughter had something particular about it. It was shrill, abrupt and lacked mirth... When he had gone around the circle, he gave a gracious nod to all assembled there and departed. It could be seen on

*Court ceremonial was strict and some
objected to having to "kiss the hand of
a man".*

71

the face of each one as to whether he had enjoyed one of the grades of fortune and if that which he had enjoyed met with his expectations..."

But intellectual life at Court was not particularly "brilliant", either at the Palace or at the Chinese Pavilion. Those nearest to the King were, in the main, "young, noble, handsome officers whose level of education seems to have been somewhat indifferent". It was a group of people where Armfelt was one of the exceptions and Hedvig Charlotta writes in her diary that there had in fact begun "to be a dearth of agreeable people in this small and tedious community, now that so many have withdrawn, worn out by the assembly of ill-educated and unpolished young men with whom the King surrounds himself and who have made the atmosphere in Court circles extremely bad".

Many of the criticisms made against Gustav III and his courtly life arose from the growing opposition against him, not least among the higher nobility. The picture painted by tradition, helped along by writers such as Tegnér, a picture of brilliant courtly life, a ferment of intellectual activity, charming as a Watteau painting, is significantly exaggerated. Superficiality, envy and intrigue were tangible realities behind the façade of the strict Court protocol, even out at the Chinese Pavilion.

An account from the 18th Century gives an international perspective to the Chinese Pavilion. In 1775, the Englishman Wraxall published a travelogue about his journeys to Northern Europe. He had worked for the English East India Company and knew the architectural "chinoiserie" better than most and was also knowledgeable as regarded many objects exported from China. "In the garden", he wrote "the Queen Dowager has recently built a small pleasure palace in a half-circle, consisting of a number of rooms decorated in the style we normally call Chinese... But I have had the great pleasure of visiting this small isolated refuge, which, owing to its large number of curios, catches the attention of the traveller more than anything else in the Realm".

After his Italian journey, in 1783 and 1784, Gustav III began to take a greater interest in Haga pleasure palace and the Classical style. The little Rococo pavilion in the grounds of Drottningholm was not used as much as before, and when the King was murdered it fell into oblivion and the gardens round about slowly became overgrown. There was the occasional, sporadic visit by the Royal Family as when Karl XIV Johan dined at the Confidence in 1823, or when Oscar I had his headquarters there in June 1845, when the Stockholm Garrison were exercising on Lovön.

But the Bernadotte family were to rescue the Pavilion from neglect and decay. Damp and rot were beginning to take their toll, but at the turn of the century, Oscar II intervened. Damaged areas of wall were replaced, the more valuable furniture was repainted and objets d'art

The Sentry Tent by the Chinese Pavilion

were taken to the Royal Palace in Stockholm to prevent further damage.

The Chinese Pavilion of today is the result of extensive restoration work, not least owing to the interest of Gustav VI Adolf. The exterior was restored between 1943 and 1955 under the leadership of the Palace Architect Ivar Tengbom, while the restoration of the interior was begun in 1959 and ready in 1968. The then Chief Curator of the Royal Art Collections, Åke Setterwall, and his successor, Stig Fogelmarck, are responsible for the consummate result. The restoration was carried out at the expense of Knut and Alice Wallenberg and was facilitated as regards furniture and objets d'art by the detailed inventory that was drawn up when Lovisa Ulrica handed over the Palace to the Crown, in 1777. Many of the original objects have been restored to their original locations of two hundred years before and this contributes to the unique quality of the Pavilion.

Queen Lovisa Ulrica's jewel beyond Flora Rise has been re-created lovingly and skillfully. Like a greeting from a distant, yet near, 18th Century. A greeting from the Rococo, from another era. Far away and yet very much present, if you stop and listen. A page from a diary, written on a sunny summer's day in 1767, gives us a living picture:

"To China, a little pleasure palace in the vicinity, the Royal Family betook themselves each day at noon, with a few specially selected persons. The rest of the Court went there of an afternoon. The more gentlemanly carried the embroidering frames. The women had enough to occupy themselves with. The King turned, the Queen listened to her reader and the Crown Prince drew, all in the same room. The Princesses made lace, Prince Karl sailed a frigate and Prince Fredrik ran about the field while the watchman smoked tobacco."

If you lie in the grass near the Chinese Pavilion on a day in high summer and close your eyes with the sun shining on your face, it is not hard to imagine the sound of happy laughter drifting through from another century and smell the fragrant tobacco of the watchman. A family idyll, far away from ceremonial and etiquette. A beautiful summer's day, where the dark blue thundercloud of politics has been banished to beyond the horizon.

The Gods of Antiquity in Leafy Groves

As I sit on the steps of the Palace and look out over the gardens and the park I take in many centuries of art history and currents of ideas. Straight ahead, on the longitudinal axis of the almost geometrically set out, strictly formal Baroque Garden, stands the sculpture of Hercules, the fountain made by de Vries, a trophy from the Thirty Years' War. The giant who raises his bronze club at the dragon, surrounded by four women symbolising the four seasons, once guarded Wallenstein's palace in Prague. More recently, he came from Ulriksdal, brought from there by Hedvig Eleonora to Drottningholm. The Hercules statue reminded her of a similar one at her childhood home, the castle at Gottorp. It took a year of labour to get the statue in place in the boggy ground, but in 1687 Hercules was in position. The workmen who had worked in a "violent shower of rain" received "by gracious order of Her Royal Majesty the recompense of a cask of beer". It was thus that the hero of antiquity, Hercules of the Twelve Labours, came to the Baroque Garden, toasted in beer. A meeting of cultures. Though he is not the only war trophy in the fountain. Three of the female figures on the dolphins around him were taken from the courtyard of Fredriksborg Castle in Denmark. The fourth, complete with amorini, also arrived via Denmark.

A glimmer of white can be seen over the powerful Baroque sculpture, *The Goddess of Flowers, Flora*
among the greenery of Muncken Rise, far beyond the patterns of box
trees and the pruned, leafy rectangles of the boscage. It is Castor and
Pollux, a marble copy of the famous Roman sculpture group modelled
on a Late Greek prototype. Desprez, both artist and architect, had, on
the suggestion of Gustav III, drawn plans for a temple that was to
frame the group, but this was never built. The original is to be found at
the Prado, in Madrid. It was once owned by Queen Christina, daughter of Gustavus II Adolphus, she who abdicated in order to convert to
Catholicism and move to Rome. In a straight line through the Baroque
Garden, we can see the sculpture from Gustavus II Adolphus' Thirty
Years' War, taken from the foremost general of the enemy as war
booty, and Castor and Pollux serve in the background as a reminder of
his daughter's love of things Classical. Her collection of statues num-
bered over 150 items. But she not only deserted Protestantism and
Sweden, but also took with her irreplaceable art treasures which were
dispersed and disappeared.

It is no coincidence that the Roman-Hellenistic group of statues can
be seen over the cascades of Kronan, the central pond, glittering in the
sun, against the spring-green background. Gustav III was the uniting

76

Neptune on guard with his trident, facing the lake.

link; it was he who placed the gods of antiquity in their burgeoning Swedish spring setting. On the rise on which Castor and Pollux stand, cowslips, wild chervil and harebells flower. The yellow buttercups of the summer meadow shine against the white of Roman marble.

After the relative darkness of the Middle Ages came the spring light of the Renaissance and the newly-awakened interest for Greece and Rome, for art and culture, swept through Europe. The exquisite sculpture of Antiquity was seen as a synthesis, summing up the Classical Golden Age of humanity. In the 16th century it became fashionable to collect sculptures. It was a fashion that spread out from Rome over the rest of the world. Kings, princes and statesmen were all collectors of art. François I of France, the contemporary of Gustav Vasa, was one, but their interests were not entirely the same. While the French King was collecting art and Antique sculpture, Gustav Vasa was busy melting down the silver treasures of the monasteries. He was not troubled by cultural scruples. What the Church had collected by way of libraries and treasuries over the centuries was effectively dispersed; a cultural, historical and intellectual setback to the development of the country that took centuries to repair. Among collectors, Cardinal Richelieu and Queen Christina were also to be found. A great deal of her collection consisted of war trophies, though a part was destroyed when the Royal Castle of Stockholm burnt down in 1697. But not only originals were collected. Casts were also made and many copies were produced. A typical example is Castor and Pollux, which was not a direct copy of the original, but made from a copy at Versailles.

Sculptures were not solely considered as collector's items and transmitters of aesthetic experience. They were also the prototype for "good art" especially as regards the proportions of the human body, and sculptures were regarded as expressing "noble" feelings. This way of thinking influenced artists of the day in cultural circles all over Europe, not least in Sweden. Tessin the Younger said that he bought them for two reasons: "For the sake of good taste and to inspire the young in their studies". Nor did his words fall on deaf ears. Both Charles XI and Charles XII brought sculptures home to Sweden.

With Gustav III, a new interest arose in the Classical heritage in Sweden. It was also an international phenomenon of the time. Excavations had been begun on the buried cities of Pompeii and Herculaneum, which had lain in the silence of the grave since the eruption of Vesuvius in 79 A.D. A wave of "enthusiasm" swept through Europe at the discovery of these new stylistic ideals, which had only just survived the Renaissance particularly in the Classical French tragedies. And two hundred years ago, at Christmas 1783, Gustav III came on a visit to Rome as the Duke of Haga. One of the reasons for coming was to buy sculptures for the planned sculpture gallery at the palace at Haga Park, a palace only the foundations of which were ever laid. Though the gallery exists in the form of the museum of Antiquity at the Royal Palace in Stockholm.

In the New Year, the King was received by Pope Pius VI who showed him the Vatican collection of sculptures. The visit is recorded by a painting in the Museum of Antiquity at the Royal Palace in Stockholm. The King and the Pope in the middle, surrounded by their entourage, with Antique statues around the walls. Armfelt has written about the visit: "The 1st January we proceeded *par ordres* wearing court dress to the Sistine Chapel *en cérémonie*. We endured, standing and kneeling, the whole rite of damnation at the entrance door, whereafter we went up to the museum and made a tour of those rooms which the present Pope was having put in order and those he had already had arranged. As we made to go, His Holiness came at full speed with priests and crucifix and showed the King personally, as if he were a librarian, not only the rooms where we had been, but also the whole library, and showed us all there was to see. The old man was charming, and at three o'clock we parted company."

The background to these collections lay in the fact that Pius' predecessor, Clement XIV, had grown concerned by the export of Antique statues. Assisted by his future successor, he had started a collection that had become one of the largest. The two prelates had succeeded in stemming the flow of culture abroad. But not every Pope shared their aesthetic interests. One of the occupants of the papal throne decreed that the statues of the Vatican were to be furnished with fig-leaves.

The sculptor, Sergel, was one of the King's retinue, though, as a commoner, he was obliged to eat at a separate table. Much later it was said that with him "New Classicism made its brilliant entry". But it had taken its time. In a letter dated 1797, Sergel writes of his first visit to Rome, thirty years previously, and describes his despair at having wasted the years of his youth without having understood the importance of the Classical world for "le vrai goût". Classical antiquity was a source of artistic inspiration when trying to reach the innermost essence of the beauty of nature.

A meeting of cultures

Sergel was artistic adviser to Gustav III when the latter made his purchases. The son of another great artist, Piranesi, was engaged as agent, the father having contributed to interest in the Classical world with his copper-plate engravings. An unscrupulous trade flourished. Excavations were made at Hadrian's villa at Tivoli and at other sites, and whatever was dug up was sold. As well as copies, Gustav III took home with him vases, sepulchral monuments, other antiques and objects d'art. On the stairs to the National Museum, the painter Carl Larsson depicts the King's enthusiasm for Classical sculpture. But there is another side to the coin. Spiteful tongues at the Italian Courts satirised the King and his purchases: "Il conte di Haga, chi molte vede, e poco paga." The Count of Haga, who bought much and paid

little also met with criticism back home, in Sweden. The journey to Italy was seen as a pleasure trip where large sums of money were squandered, sums that could have found better use in a poor country, such as Sweden. Disaffection was rife in Sweden and the leading politician, Count Scheffer wrote: "I would fain give up all I possess to be able to cancel this journey."

The journey also had immediate consequences for the introduction of the Classical style to Sweden. While in Italy, Gustav III halted building work on the Church of St. John (Johanneskyrkan) in Stockholm. The King now preferred to have a Roman Panthéon. He also engaged the gifted Frenchman, Louis Jean Desprez. Desprez was both artist and architect and, as mentioned above, he was to be of great importance to the Court Theatre through his contribution of the decorations. He was also the architect of the never-completed Haga Castle, a grandiose Roman temple the King had thought to build in Haga Park. Only grass-covered ruins remain of the proud dreams of the Golden Age of Classicism. But other vestiges are still in evidence. The Breakfast Lounge at the Court Theatre, the Gothic Tower and Vilan, all at Drottningholm, as well as the stage-scenery copper tent at Haga and the Chinese Pavilion. The temple-like façade of Botanicum in Upsala, echoed in that of the University Library, Carolina Rediviva, are two further expressions of his artistry. "In this country, there are only two persons of any imagination", said Gustav III. "Me, and Desprez." But the gold of royal grace turned to that of fools after the shot at the Opera. With the King's death, Desprez lost a powerful patron and died a pauper.

In 1777, the same year as he took over Drottningholm, Gustav III had already worked out a plan for an English garden, "Plan du Nouveau Jardin à l'Anglais". This covered the area not already taken up by the Baroque Garden. I can therefore look out from the steps of the Palace over three different dimensions of landscape. Furthest away, in the South West, stand the woods, the disciplined wilderness of dishevelled pine and spruce beyond Flora Rise. Straight ahead lies the formal, French Baroque Garden around which the romantically irregular English Garden stretches.

Like so much else during the course of history, the English Garden was a reaction. In this case, against the artificiality of the Baroque Garden. The corset required by tradition and etiquette was removed from nature. Originally it was inimical and threatening. Mankind struggled for existence, a struggle against a hostile environment. The forest loomed threateningly around cultivated clearings. Wild beasts with shining eyes crept silently under the overhanging branches, while the ancient gods had been turned by the Catholic Church into giants and trolls as they crouched hollow-eyed behind moss-covered Ice Age rocks which they vainly cast at the white churches of the plains. Nature was to be approached gradually. It had to be disciplined and tamed. The hymn-writer and archbishop Haquin Spegel sums up the Caroline interpretation of "The Open Paradise" when he writes:

> To make of wilderness a pleasure garden,
> Proves that one is of country honour warden.

His ideal was Versailles where man had succeeded in taming nature, compelling it to submit:

> What Paradise looked like, one gladly shews there
> Yea; show what kind of might France doth bear
> There must be rocky hills and generous springs
> there must be woods and water marsh and groves and other things.

Spegel also described the park at Drottningholm:

> Its wall is uncommon, its plain full even and wide,
> And has statues, also fountains on every side.

Landscape gardening thus became part of the pacification of a hostile environment, and the French Baroque Garden was a trend-setting step on the way. Nature was conquered and disciplined, rendered harmless and made to obey Man's will and the etiquette of the Court. The walls surrounding it were a bulwark against the environment outside of the geometrical patterns of the central axis which is at right angles to the longitudinal axis of the main buildings, and the parterre is divided up into quarters with fountains placed at the intersections.

The English Garden was the next step. The walls of the garden were demolished in line with the Rococo wish and Rousseau's desire to return to Nature, but a Nature suited to Man and formed by him. There was a reaction against architectonic compositions with pruned bushes and pollarded trees. Nature was idealised, animated and was to give rest, relaxation and inspiration. Paths wound their way through the gentle landscape of decidious trees, where small grottoes, pavilions and other pleasant surprises waited in the bushes. A clearing opens out suddenly among the trees, a stream pearls and the branches of trees are reflected in ponds. Pillars of a temple rise up in the background. Here too, the Chinese influence on Rococo can be felt. This was brought not least by the Swedish-born Englishman, William Chambers, in his work "A Dissertation on Oriental Gardening", which he presented to Gustav III and in return received the Order of Vasa. One of the lasting results of the influence of Chambers is Kew Gardens in London.

The former marshland became a romantic series of ponds.

Gustav III was to use a number of his sculptures in the English Park. Instead of romantic grottoes and other features the King put up marble statues from Rome. He followed two principles. They were to be seen among the foliage and, as with the Baroque Garden, they were to be the end focus of long perspectives. That is why Castor and Pollux shine up there through the green foliage on the hillside in the distance.

But the King's plans for the English Park were not drawn up overnight. The Baroque Garden in front of the Palace was the fruit of long and painstaking labour. At first, when Johan III built the original Palace in 1579 for his Queen, Katarina Jagiellonica, there was no park at all. Nor were there any grounds save the "utility garden" looked after by the "gardiner", Bengt and his three hands. It lay to the North of the Palace. To the West, where the Baroque and English Gardens now lie, there was a deer park, right up to the walls of the courtyard, where the King amused himself with deer-hunting. Even though, for the sake of the hunt, certain thinning and clearing had taken place, the deer park was largely untouched wilderness. The area was also marshy and water-logged, an excellent breeding ground for gnats which were

81

considered "more virulent" than in many other places, and the dreaded Drottningholm ague rose out of the alder marsh where the ponds now lie.

The Drottningholm of Johan III burnt down and it was not until 1662, the year after the fire, that Hedvig Eleonora began to take an interest in creating a park for the new Palace. Nicodemus Tessin the Elder was the architect and it was part of his task to make a pleasure garden out of the old deer park. Also Magnus Gabriel De la Gardie, during the short time he devoted to Drottningholm, had plans to make a terrace between the Palace and Lake Mälaren, but the plans were never realised.

Trees were felled, the ground was drained in its most marshy parts and levelled. The gardens envisaged by the Queen were, by and large, those that I am looking out over today from the steps in front of the Palace. A broad avenue running straight towards Muncken Rise. Geometrically uniform areas, parterres with hedges of box trees face one another along the wide centre avenue, where the end part of the background consisted of four boscages or hedge labyrinths. Half way along, a pond was to be found and on both sides of the garden an avenue of limes was planted.

Nicodemus Tessin the Elder, and later his son, produced various plans before the Queen Dowager was satisfied. The garden, as it was finally to become, is an offshot of French Baroque. The basic influence originates with the Frenchman, André le Nôtre, who had created gardens at Vaux-le-Vicomte, the Tuileries, Chantilly and those at Versailles. Later research considers that le Nôtre even might have had a hand in drawing up the original plans. The gardens were modernised by Tessin the Younger, who brought back many impulses from his travels abroad. His fundamental philosophy can be summarised in one sentence: "The greatest science when planning a garden is to know and examine well the drawbacks and advantages of the area, so that one can profit from the latter, yet correct the former."

In "Beskrifning öfver Upland" (Description of Upland) of 1741 we can read about the garden at Drottningholm: "This pleasure garden comprises a large space with many lovely decidious trees, along with barberry, juniper and pine which have been pruned to form hedges and pyramids and various ornaments... Here too we find many kinds of running water made into designs..."

Many technical problems remained to be solved, not least the water supply. In the pond in the centre of the garden, "Kronan", the crown, there was a fountain, "like a mountain of water", behind which lay the Cascades, a wall with running water right across the garden, which did not actually function until the 1950s when it was restored on the initiative of Gustav IV Adolf. The water was supplied to the ponds by means of a pipe constructed by a French "fountain-maker". The pipes

consisted of hollowed-out tree trunks connected to one another by pushing the narrow end of the one trunk into the broader end of the next. The 875 tree trunks had been transported from Gripsholm. Those pipes that were preserved and were discovered during excavations can be found in the cellar of the Chinese Pavilion to this day. They never worked particularly well, but today it has become easier. The water for the fourteen ponds with fountains, as well as that for the Cascades and Kronan pours forth without hindrance and the bronze dragon on the Hercules Fountain throws its jet of water high into the blue sky.

Near the Chinese Pavilion there is also a Baroque-style garden. This was laid out by Lovisa Ulrica. From the Pavilion, avenues radiate to the four points of the compass. The one running eastwards goes up to Flora Rise, and is surrounded by boscage "serving to create an intimate atmosphere", which made the whole design lighter in tone and less pompous than the large garden.

That was what the French pleasure garden looked like when Gustav III took over the Palace in 1777 and planned his English Park. But there were still problems, not least with the marshy "Träsket", to the North of the Baroque Garden, where the ponds now lie. One descrip-

83

tion states that "the Northern part of the present gardens was completely flooded".

It took a visionary, such as Gustav III to create an English park peopled with marble statues out of waterlogged ground, marsh and bushes, even though his plans were not carried through. He set about the task with great energy. The marsh to the South of the Palace was drained by means of a canal which ran out to the West of the Chinese Pavilion. The King's plans were ambitious. Bridges were to be built over the canal, avenues were to be planted, new boscages were to be created and monuments, in the form of ruins, castles and temples were to be raised on high ground. And at the end of the Baroque Garden a "Temple de Gloire" was to be built. But as always, compromises had to be made.

Gustav III consulted the architect Fredrik Magnus Piper, who had been educated in England, and the result of the King's plans and Piper's skill is the gentle, idyllic landscape around the formal Baroque Garden. The old marsh in the North became a romantic pond with green trees and white swans which can be seen across the open grassy

The English Park as seen from the Governor's Residence.

slopes. To the South of the Palace we can see a system of canals filled with water lilies under tall trees. Around 15,000 trees and bushes were bought specially for the English Park from England and Germany. Piper also became "ordonnateur", developing the park at Haga in the same romantic spirit.

A little maliciously, Ehrensvärd writes that Gustav III asked Sergel what he thought of the English Park which was under construction. Ingenuously Sergel answered: "I saw the most beautiful English garden more than twelve years ago before I left Sweden. Your Majesty owns it, it is Fiskartorpet on his own estate on the island of Djurgården." The King did clearly not appreciate the comparison, for as Ehrensvärd mentions: "The conversation ceased on that topic."

As I sit on the steps, the roof of a red brick tower can be seen along the lime avenue. It is the Gothic Tower, a knight's castle with loopholes near the top, a romantic project which Gustav III carried out. It is octagonal and designed by Desprez, the same architect that created the Breakfast Lounge adjoining the Court Theatre which turns its Classical face towards the grassy slope by the ponds. The romantic tower was never used for anything practical but stands there as a piece of scenery to fill the onlooker with noble thoughts of days gone by and as an illustration of an interesting episode in the long history of Drottningholm. Though it was used once. On the birthday of Crown Prince Gustav Adolf, a greeting was sent to the Palace in Stockholm by optical telegraph.

Another monument, though incomplete, lies in the vicinity of the tower, on Monument Mound. Here we can find a cairn forming the plinth to a monument of Gustav III. From the mound, lime avenues radiate like the stays of a fan.

A summary of the development of the park at Drottningholm was made at the beginning of the 19th Century. "Art has exerted itself here to conquer nature. The area where the beautiful garden now lies, formerly marshy and waterlogged, has with arches of stone covered with much soil been transformed into a dry level plain. Rocks have been blasted or covered with earth and turf so that they now resemble green hills; clumps of trees have been tied up and trimmed and the hillsides decorated with deciduous trees; the paths have been gravelled, all the marshy areas have been filled in, the fens and stagnant water intersected by wide canals or drained by means of brick outlets; a street of pretty stone houses has taken the place of the former hovels."

The temple and most of the other romantic "props" were never built in Gustav III's English Park. But the statues were set in place. Near Castor and Pollux, there originally stood a faun with a goat over his shoulder. The original had, in the same way as Castor and Pollux, belonged to Queen Christina and ended up in the Prado Gallery, in Madrid. But the faun did not get on with his surroundings. The statue was damaged by the rainwater that fell through the dense foliage of the surrounding trees and it had to be moved to a more open spot. The faun with his pipes of Pan was placed up on the road to Ekerö, near the Monument Mound. Mars, the God of War was also to be found there, against a background of tall trees near the ponds. In 1958 the statue was restored and Mars was relieved of his many centuries old fig-leaf. A little further up, near Canton hamlet, sits Ares. Like Mars, he came to Sweden on the frigate "Bellona".

The faun was not the only statue that had to be protected from rain and sap from foliage. This was also the case with the four statues in the Philosophers' Grove in the northern part of the English Park, right beside the road to Ekerö island, near the carrousel area, where Gustav III and his Court held their tournaments. In 1955, a committee of experts under the chairmanship of Gustav VI Adolf, decided that they were to be put in a less exposed place. The Farnese Hercules, Antinous, Germanicus and Demosthenes now stand down by the waterside in front of the Palace and look over Lake Mälaren with their dead, marble eyes.

Where the village of Glia once lay, the knights' stronghold of the Gothic Tower rises above the foliage. A romantic exclamation mark in Gustav III's English Park.

Mars and Venus by Adriaen de Vries

Hercules was a popular subject during ancient times and there are many copies in existence. As has already been mentioned, the Farnese Hercules is not alone at Drottningholm. The Hercules by de Vries stands in the fountain in the Baroque Garden, and in a niche in the façade of the Palace there is a copy of a Hercules that had belonged to Queen Christina.

Antinous, next to Hercules on the lake shore, was much loved by Hadrian, but came to a tragic end. He drowned in the Nile in 130 A.D. Antinous belonged to the statues which Napoleon had taken from Rome to the Louvre and the Englishman, William Hogarth, wrote in his "Analysis of Beauty" that Antinous was the most perfect of all Greek statues. He talks of the extreme beauty of its proportions.

Next to Antinous stands Germanicus, which Sergel admired greatly. He considered Germanicus an extraordinary synthesis of "a great and noble statesman", and he copied it from a prototype in the collections of the King of France. Sergel used the prototype for his statue of Axel Oxenstierna and the Muse of History.

Last in line, nearest the Palace, follows the orator, Demosthenes. It was originally named "the Philosopher" and was valued at 200 Rixdollars in Gustav III's inventory. The original stands in the Vatican. My children irreverently call the row of lightly clad statues "the Great Parade of Bottoms".

But the most charming statue at Drottningholm is Diana, Goddess of the Hunt. She stands with her dog on a little holm among the ponds, and rises over the pale meadowsweet of the lake shore. One hand is raised over her head, either to shade her eyes or to take an arrow from the quiver on her back. Just now she is absent for a time. Her head has been knocked off and one arm has vanished, the victim of hooligans early one summer's morning near the end of the school term. A brutal confrontation between cultural depravity and the values of the Ancients. Now the vandalism has spread. Four statues have been desecrated and damaged. A premeditated outrage, for who carries on their person a hammer and chisel into the grounds of Drottningholm? But Mars and the faun with his flute will return.

Outside the Breakfast Lounge of the Court Theatre there are two Egyptian lions, the only Roman sculptures where one can see that the original intention has been followed. We read in the King's inventory, "2 Egyptian lions for the new salon, from Italy, 50 Rixdollars each". They give an exotic touch to the Classical façade and the children who ride on their white backs do not realise that almost the same lions guard the Capitol in Rome. From an art point of view, these two lions belong to the most interesting purchases made by Gustav III in Italy.

Further away from the Palace there are also sculptures. In the boscage we find Apollo with his lyre, to good effect placed at the end of the open-air theatre with its green hedges. Performances are still given here. It was described as a place where "Masquerades, Festive Entertainments, Ballets, Concerts, Illuminations and similar Activities can take place". And the actors change between scenes in the labyrinth of dark green hedges as before.

The same lion guards the Capitol in Rome.

Group of bronzes in the Baroque Garden by Adriaen de Vries.

To the South of Apollo, we find the goddess Flora, at the top of Flora Rise and planned as a *point de vue* from the Chinese Pavilion. At first, Flora stood on Muncken Rise but was moved and replaced by Castor and Pollux, as she was not sufficiently large to be seen clearly from the Baroque Garden. The original was found in the thermae of Marcus Aurelius, in 1540.

But it was not only Gustav III who set up sculptures in the park. Hedvig Eleonora had the Hercules Fountain built by de Vries. Around thirty other bronze figures can be found at Drottningholm, war trophies from Prague and Denmark, obtained during the 17th Century. Mars and Venus still embrace in patinated green, while Amor looks discreetly away and Mercury runs across the courtyard towards the two wrestlers. Venus and Bacchus can be found down in the Baroque Garden. Facing Lake Mälaren stands Neptune with his Trident, defying unwelcome visitors. But originally there were more. Ulrica Eleonora the Younger gave, as a contribution to the casting of the new bell for the church at Munsö, "a number of old statues and figures made of metal which once stood in the pleasure gardens at Drottningholm". And Tessin had melted down a large Renaissance group in bronze, when he needed the metal for the large lion on Slottsbacken outside the Royal Palace in Stockholm.

It has been said that de Vries' figures were "not the best that sculpture has to offer" and that they were created as decoration to be seen from afar. "They do not stand up to closer examination." But I consider them to be a priceless and charming contribution to the gardens, giving life and energy to the austere landscape of box trees.

The Queen Dowager also had erected the marvellous gates on the North Avenue. Without being a sculpture, Hårleman's Baroque gates with Hedvig Eleonora's monogram under the Royal Crown hold their own among the decorative elements in the park.

Following the murder of Gustav III in 1792, interest in Drottningholm gradually waned. The Royal Family favoured other pleasure palaces and the grounds fell into neglect, the park grew over. The box tree parterres became lawns, the water parterres were shut off. Kronan, the large pond with the fountain, was removed and the cascades became grassy slopes. Trees grew and hid the façade on the Mälar side. "The neat French Garden is far from what it used to be" a 19th Century writer states.

Not until the time of Gustav V and Viktoria of Baden did the park and gardens undergo a renaissance when the Palace was renovated at the beginning of the 20th Century. But it was written, as late as in the Twenties that: "Of the many grand features of the park, only the foundations remain. Many of the finest details have been lost and the appearance of the gardens has, at times, been simplified to the point of unrecognisability. On the initiative of the present Queen, reconstruction based on the original plan has begun."

The work was completed by Gustav VI Adolf with the support of Professors Ivar Tengbom and Nils Wallin as well as the landscape architect, Walter Bauer. It is to them we owe credit for the fact that the Baroque Garden at Drottningholm has been restored to its original state and that it is now one of the best examples of its type outside France, as well as for the restoration of Gustav III's romantic English Park.

A cloud blocks out the sun, it grows chilly. A sudden omen of autumn. I rise to go, stroll slowly along the crunching gravel towards the Court Theatre. And there, with the pale yellow theatre building as backdrop, stands the Apollo Belvedere in marble. Wreathed in laurel, with one arm outstretched, beckoning. He too is a copy of an original bronze figure from 400 B.C. But Apollo came to Sweden long before Gustav III's Italian journey. As early as 1698, the statue was sent, along with other sculptures, in wooden crates from France, presumably by order of Nicodemus Tessin the Younger. It was also this statue that was rated highest in Gustav III's inventory, at 400 Rixdollars.

Many sculptors and artists have been inspired by the Apollo Belvedere, which was seen as one of the high points of Classical sculpture. William Hogarth wrote that Apollo had "an appearance of something more than human" and others, such as Ehrenstrahl and Sergel, were equally enthusiastic.

Apollo, the Sun God, who was also patron of poetry, art and music, has been interpreted as a personification of Gustav III. Sergel's statue of him on Skeppsbron in Stockholm does not gainsay this interpretation. For me it is not hard to agree. Apollo is the only one of the marble statues that has been placed centrally, up in the courtyard which is an integral part of the Palace grounds. In his perfection, he stands there as a personification of the Classifical heritage, in front of the austere façade of the Court Theatre. What can better represent Gustav III's contribution to Drottningholm, the King who, despite all his eccentricity and aestheticising, nevertheless brought the sun of culture from the Mediterranean up over the spiky horizons of the Swedish forest. Without him Sweden would undoubtedly have been the poorer today. "A certain brilliance lay over the days of Gustav", as Tegnér put it, and for Sergel the King was "a ray of heavenly light". And this was no mere conversation piece from the salons of Court flattery, he said this long after Gustav III had passed away. A Swedish Apollo could have been judged worse.

Like a Bach fugue in a shaft of light, the stairs rise upwards.

As in a Bottle of Green Glass

I enter the Palace by the main entrance on the lake side, guarded by white marble lions, and step under the large coat-of-arms of the Queen Dowager which almost covers the roof of the porch, framed by cornucopiae and wreaths. The wind carries towards me the heavy, rich scent of the limes flowering in the avenues. Inside, it is cool. Silent and cool. I leave one world and step into another. Outside, the faint hum of traffic can be heard from the bridge beyond the curtain of sound provided by the birds and the summer breeze, but here inside, where all is silence, we are in another epoch. As in a bottle of green glass where the world outside can be seen through the vitreous bulge, but distorted and distant. The cool, the dusk, the scents and echoes of voices from the mists of time. Or is this all in my imagination, am I a victim of moods and impressions when I stand at the end of a vista and look out through a portal in the distance, out over the park, through a miniature colonnade, an "allée" of Doric pillars. This is a typical trait of the Baroque style of architecture; creating an illusion with perspectives and planes. A similar vista was to be found at the castle of Gottorp, the childhood home of the Queen.

I go up into the lower vestibule, stand on the stone floor with my back to the Baroque Garden out there in the sunshine, and look at Hedvig Eleonora's staircase in front of me. It rises in splendid Baroque style towards the floor above like a Bach fugue in a shaft of light.

Drottningholm, like many palaces, has its own story and I have told about some of the things that occurred here and about some of the participants. As regards architecture and design too, there are many different stages, different epochs. Nicodemus Tessin the Elder left his mark on the former when he began as architect to the Queen Dowager, in 1662. The next stage was reached when his son, Nicodemus Tessin the Younger, took over on the death of his father in 1681. He was said to personify "more than any other artist, Swedish dreams of power during the Caroline era". He studied French, Italian and English at Upsala, as well as mathematics and architecture. At the age of nineteen, he made a study visit to the Continent, and in Rome he came into contact with the great Italian architect, Bernini, thanks to the good offices of Queen Christina. Nicodemus also visited France where he was impressed by the Louvre and Versailles as well as the lancscape architecture of Le Nôtre. Like his father before him, he became architect both to the Palace and to the City of Stockholm. After the fire in 1697, he drew plans for a new Palace and was created a Count and a Marshal in Chief and took part in an architectural competition for the rebuilding of the Louvre. He brought new ideas and impulses to Swedish architecture, not least concerning the interior of Drottningholm. At the time of the death of his father, the exterior was more or less completed. Only the Chapel Royal remained to be built.

From the light Swedish summer, one steps into the heavy, pompous Baroque of the 17th Century, where art glorified the Royal power. Straight ahead is the magnificent staircase which flows upwards in stone and marble. In the illustrated work, "Suecia Antiqua", which was brought into being for reasons of propaganda to show Sweden as a great power, we find a copper-plate engraving of a cutaway section of the stair-well. The Latin text proudly proclaims that its like is to be found nowhere in Europe. And this was intentional. Sweden was, after all, a great power and this fact was meant to be seen and noticed. Or, as someone wrote about the Palace at Drottningholm: "It is the character of our time of Swedish greatness that shines forth, the character of a time when one, in all seriousness, sought to make Sweden the cradle of cultivation and the home of creation, and it is the stamp of this epoch that we call the Baroque period, which here, sharply and in chiselled form, sees the light of day."

The Italian, Carove, made the ornamentation of the ceiling and the walls in stucco – hard plaster – in the Lower Vestibule, following the drawings made by Tessin. It cost 170 Rixdollars in specie and the paintings on the ceiling, in the style of a triumphal Roman procession,

Lintel in the Marble Cabinet

was painted by the Swedish artist, Johan Sylvius. He was working in England after studying in Italy and receiving orders from the Vatican, when he was summoned to Sweden by Hedvig Eleonora, in 1685. A great deal had been heard about Sylvius. The Swedish Ambassador in London reported that he "has worked out at Windsor... and he has been praised for his great sobriety, which is, among great artists, a rare quality". Sylvius was also aware of his worth. Charles XI thought that he asked too much for his services. The fee was the equivalent of the salary of a colonel. To this, Sylvius replied: "Your Majesty can appoint 20 colonels in one day, but he could not find another Sylvius in 20 years."

On either side of the Lower Vestibule lie the Northern and Southern Halls of the Lifeguards. The décor is less lavish, with painted imitation stucco ceilings. In the Northern Hall, there is interesting wallpaper in gilt leather, which depicts the siege of Vienna by the Turks, in 1683. For us, it is history, but for the contemporary world it was a propagandistic piece of reportage from the world out there in Europe, where the threat of Turkish dominance was a living reality throughout the centuries. There are also painting by the Court painter, David Klöcker Ehrenstrahl, who, along with Sylvius, was responsible for much of the artistic decoration of the Palace. One large canvas depicts a dromedary led by a man in a turban. But this has nothing whatsoever to do with Charles XII's sojourn in Bender. The dromedary belonged to Charles XI and in his accounts from the year 1689, there is an item of expenditure entitled: "new stablehand's uniform for the Turk who looks after the camels in Our stable." He was a Royal stable hand, by the name of Schabasch, but was christened Nils in the Castle Chapel in Stockholm, after Nils Bielke who had sent him, along with the dromedary, to the King. Bielke had brought Schabasch home from the wars against the Turks, in which Swedish officers also took part. What Schabasch himself thought of being christened Nils and looking after camels in snowy Sweden is not mentioned.

Ehrenstrahl, who was German, began his Swedish career as a clerk in the Swedish Chancellory during the peace negotiations at Osnabrück, in connection with the Thirty Years' War. He is responsible for many glorious paintings at Drottningholm, but fate would have it that he also came to paint animals, besides kings, queens and generals. The Queen's dogs was a motif that often recurred. One year, he made seven "portraits" of the dog Courtisan. He also painted horses: Sultan, Pegasus, Precieux, Tott and several others. In the end, he became sick and tired of portraying animals. In a letter to Erik Dahlberg, who not only led Charles X over the frozen surface of the Great Belt, during the war against the Danes, but who was also the guiding light behind "Suecia Antiqua", complained bitterly and hoped that an end would soon come to this "miserable portraiture of miserable animals". A "real" artist in those days would paint large canvases with allegorical scenes showing important figures. Animal painting was not highly regarded. Ironically, Ehrenstrahl would go down in history as one of the pioneers of animal painting, and a forerunner of Bruno Liljefors. His "Capercaillies Courting", painted at Kungsör in 1676, was one of the first Swedish landscapes with animals in realistic surroundings.

From the Northern Hall of the Lifeguards with its heavy Baroque, I enter the Green Salon. Green damask covers the walls and the room is of interest not least because it unites the "great" epochs. The doors are by Tessin the Elder, while the ceiling is the work of his son. The furniture is Rococo and the mirrors in the style of Gustav III. It was previously called the Velvet Room, because of the maroon tapestries which Oscar I had put up. He used it as a dining-room.

Lovisa Ulrica's parents hang on either side of Louis XV in his gold frame, which in its resplendent exuberance almost upstages the King of France. But Lovisa Ulrica was not satisfied with the portrait of her mother, Queen Sophia Dorothea of Prussia. In a letter she complains that her mother has been portrayed as *"extraordinairement engraissée"*, exceptionally fat. Catherine the Great of Russia, who hangs opposite, was also dissatisfied with her portrait. She sent the portrait back, claiming she looked like a "peasant woman". As the court artists of the time strove to beautify their models of high station, we can ask ourselves what the original looked like.

Next to the Green Salon is the Ehrenstrahl Salon. Ehrenstrahl paints large, heavy portraits of the history of the Swedish Royal Family, in the form of allegories: *"das principalste der Königlichen Historie von Anno 1660 bis 1693"*. He also circulated a description so that the paintings and his allegorical language should be understood. And this was perhaps necessary, for Ehrenstrahl wrote that a fine painting was to resemble "a subtle and well thought out puzzle". The painting which represents the Queen Dowager's Regency government has the following description:

"The Queen Dowager, Hedvig Eleonora, in her 24th year, is sitting upon a throne, clad in her purple mantle, lined with ermine. To her right, stands Faith, with a golden cross in her hand; Charity, with a child on her arm, beside her two other children that are conversing with one another; thereafter Hope, Goodliness and Honesty. These together are presenting the Queen Dowager with a portrait of her son, Charles XI, in his fifth year;... To the left of the Queen we can see a rudder inscribed with the name of Charles XI, along with his regalia. The Queen has her hand on the rudder. Righteousness, Nobility, Bravery, Prudence and Moderation, representing the five offices of the Regency, help her to steer...

Down below, to the right of the throne, stands Glory in his apparel, turned towards the Queen and gesturing towards Architecture, Painting and Sculpture, who can be seen on the left, before the throne. The first-named is presenting the Queen with plans for Drottningholm Palace, nearby sit several children who are unfurling other plans, namely those for Strömsholm, Gripsholm, Wadstena and Ulriksdal..."

It is the ageing Ehrenstrahl who wielded the brush, a weary artist, painting out of habit. Tessin makes fun of the result. The canvasses were painted under the censorship of the ladies of the Court who "hated shadow, and in whose eyes carmine and ultramarine were the only acceptable colours, pretty and kind faces the only admissible physiognomy and vivid red and white the only nuances of the face". Ehrenstrahl's "first paintings can be hung in galleries, the later ones hardly in the porch".

A more just example of Ehrenstrahl's capacity can be seen in the adjacent room, Hedvig Eleonora's State Bedchamber. With powerful compositions in living colours, he creates allegorical pictures with allusions to the Royal Family on wall panels and ceiling. The large ceiling painting shows two hands that grasp one another in a gesture of marital union. These allude to Charles X Gustav and Hedvig Eleonora.

The State Bedchamber is the most splendid room in the whole Palace and not only there. It has been said that there is not a 17th Century room in Sweden "which, in its décor, be it painting decorative sculpture or gilt and rare wood, can compare with this room".

It is the only room in the Palace which has been consistently and

minutely decorated in the Baroque style. The ceiling exhibits gilt reliefs in wood, stucco and copper-plate. The floor is a detailed puzzle of six different types of wood which reflect the divisions of the ceiling. The foremost artists of the time contributed, the sculptor Burchard Precht, the Court carpenter Meylandt, the stuccoer Carove, the sculptor Millich and many others.

At first, the State Bedchamber was almost a Hall of Memory, a manifestation of the Queen Dowager's mourning for Charles X Gustav, who died in 1660. "The decorative details were chosen to show the sorrow of the young widow at the loss of her husband, her faith in a reunion, and her hopes for her son, the Crown Prince." When the room was ready, in 1683, it was painted black, the colour of mourning. It must have given an almost macabre impression to enter the richly decorated, almost overburdened Baroque State Bedchamber painted completely in black. Not until 1701 did the mourning cease, at least as regards the colour scheme, and the Queen let the room be repainted in its present blue tones, a perfect background to the gilt details. In spite of its being the State Bedchamber, Hedvig Eleonora never slept there. It was used on official occasions, to receive ambassadors and the like, and was not equipped with a bed until 1710. It was Lovisa Ulrica who first used it as a bedroom.

I continue through the Green Cabinet, next to the State Bedchamber. This is the room that Lovisa Ulrica had Hårleman decorate completely in Rococo style, and the ladies of the Court, along with the Crown Princess, embroidered the upholstery for the Rococo furniture. She wrote that it "will become very dear to me, having *boiserie* in white and portraits of my dear family". The name of the room stems from the fact that green damask covers the walls. The room now contains a collection a pastel portraits of the Royal Family by Gustaf Lundberg, one of Sweden's leading artists of the 18th Century. Lovisa Ulrica admired Lundberg. "He was just the painter she wanted, internationally renowned and capable of reproducing the playful, glad and spiritual atmosphere of the Rococo in glowing colours." And I understand her, for the collection of portraits in the Green Cabinet is perhaps the most living and "modern" depiction of people from one certain epoch in the whole Palace. But the most beautiful portrait, the most personal, is the one in the adjoining room. It depicts Lovisa Ulrica's brother, Frederick the Great, as a child. Antoine Pesne, painter to the Prussian Court had painted it and every time I enter the Palace, I stop at this point. A child, dressed in the manner of, and indeed resembling, a little girl stands in front of a Rococo chair on which a dog is sitting. On the floor lies a toy drum and a number of flowers. The model looks the onlooker straight in the eye. For me, this canvas exemplifies what is best in Rococo painting. The colours, the lightness of touch, the spirituality and the playful elegance. If I were allowed to take with me

The Library as seen from the Marble Cabinet.

99

something from my tour of the Palace, the choice would not be difficult to make. The Queen's fine collection of art comes, to a large extent, from Carl Gustaf Tessin who had been forced to sell his treasures. He wrote in his diary of 1758: "There are two pieces of foolhardiness that I can admit to having committed. The first is my numerous collections, the second, the buildings and decorations on the islands of Åkerö and Leckö... Under the auspices of my late father, I was suckled on art, my inclination was nourished daily when I saw his collection of prints, drawings and some, though not many, paintings, of which I thought we in Sweden suffered a lack... Money I was not short of in those days. My inclination, my wealth and maybe my standing in this country as what might be called with an element of pride promoter of the arts, caused me to make numerous purchases which have allowed me to believe, and this I still do, that this and other collections, assembled by a connoisseur and with discretion, can never fall but will indeed increase in value. I again found opportunity during my last posting to France where it occured that a number of Crozats, Maréchal d' Estrées, Prince Carignans and Cabinetts were sold by public auction. Can a hungry man who has teeth and freedom be at table without eating?"

With hindsight it must be stated that Swedish artistic life would, without the hunger that Tessin displayed, be a great deal the poorer. We have good cause to be thankful to him. Much of the best work at the National Museum was obtained through his good offices, e.g. the splendid "Birth of Venus" by Boucher. This inspired Bellman to write his epistle on "The Magnificence of Venus", which begins with the words: "Blow ye all, Hear the billows swell."

A little nostalgically, Tessin sums up his years of collecting in "An Old Man's Epistle to a Young Prince" when he writes to the future Gustav III: "Let not My Gracious Sir be surprised at my dwelling so long upon the subject of paintings: a large part of those which are now kept at Drottningholm were once owned by me: Your Royal Highness need neither wonder nor muse as to the cause of their moving home. It is thus: they have gained permanent lodging and may, when I am gone, remind my Gracious Prince of the fact that I once lived."

And so comes the Library, which has been called Sweden's most beautiful room. Initially, it was intended as a picture gallery, but it became too small. It looks out over the Baroque Garden and was created by Jean Erik Rehn, following the wishes of Lovisa Ulrica when she added a storey to the wings, the floors with her monogram in iron above the windows. The Library is light, airy and the Rococo is somewhat subdued, with touches of Classicism. A fine, honey-coloured parquet floor with a geometric pattern. The décor is in gold, white and off-white and the thousands of books, bound in light calf with their titles on the spines in darkening gold, give the room a life of its own. Above the doors sit marble plaques with Latin quotations from Ovid, Horace and other Classical Romans. On one we find "Virtue lives on in the song beyond the grave". A fine summary of Lovisa Ulrica's contribution to culture. At Drottningholm her spirit lives on and traces of her works remain now that she is no longer with us.

There were, in fact, three libraries at Drottningholm. The first was created by Hedvig Eleonora and Ulrica Eleonora the Younger. The library of the Caroline queens, full of heavy, religious tomes was taken to Gripsholm and ended up, during the 19th Century, at the Royal Library in Stockholm. Later, some of the works were returned to Drottningholm. Lovisa Ulrica's library consisted almost exclusively of books in French. They covered a wide field. History, literature and illustrated works. Racine, Molière, La Fontaine and, not least, Voltaire, with dedications and annotations by the author. French and Italian drama were also represented. At various times, the Queen had both a French and an Italian ensemble. And on the shelves stand English novels by writers such as Fielding, and also Swedish literature of the type exemplified by Olof von Dalin. He was "Minister of Fun and Poet Laureate", but also the Secretary of the Academy of Learning and Historiographer of the Realm. His "Svea Rikes Historia" (The History of the Swedish Realm) is one of the most worn and read volumes, as well as, touchingly enough, Rousseau's utopian handbook on the upbringing of children, "Émile". A large collection of manuscripts from Swedish history was also to be found there.

The third library was that of Gustav III. He had a considerable book collection. At the Palace in Stockholm alone, there were nearly 15,000 volumes. His library at Drottningholm not only comprised literature but also works on law, economics, the study of nature and military matters.

Lovisa Ulrica came from an intellectual milieu, where the leading cultural figures of the time rubbed shoulders, and her library does not seem to be an expression of an aestheticising "culture", but rooted in genuine literary and cultural interest. An Englishman who visited Drottningholm at the time was surprised to find such an exquisite library, "where books in every field had been collected with good judgement, by a Queen who understood both Latin and modern tongues".

In a letter to her sister, Amalia, Lovisa Ulrica describes her study. "Here at home, at my own Drottningholm, I live like a philosopher. If you could see me at this very moment, you should find me in a room which I have set in order and where all my books stand on shelves that are recessed into the walls and furnished with glass doors; all is gilded and sculptured. The lintels are inscribed with the attributes of knowledge, over the mantelpiece hangs a mirror and under this stand Antique bronze sculptures. In the middle of the room stands a table of a completely new type from France, which contains an épergne on which there is a clock. It is at this table that I sit writing to you. Near one window, there hangs a barometer, in the other, a sundial. The last thing that I shall describe is the good armchair in which I am sitting while I make these observations. I have shut myself away, no-one may enter without my permission and I am my own master."

The above is a description of that which is now known as the Marble Cabinet, her first library, and shows her inclinations and need for intellectual stimulation.

At Drottningholm, Lovisa Ulrica held court in the literal sense of the word, when she assembled around her a circle of Sweden's foremost scientists and scholars, such as the mathematician Klingenstierna, the linguist Ihre and the geologist Tilas. Writers came here and also Carl von Linné (Linnaeus), who was given the task of organising her collections. While still Crown Princess, she had met Linnaeus, this in the same year as she came to Sweden, namely 1744. In a letter to her mother she wrote: "I have been to take a look at Linnaeus' botanical garden which is most worthy of note as it contains a collection of plants

A *Chinaman in bronze in the Coin and Medal Cabinet.*

from all the countries in the world. There are a number from China, some of which are poisonous, to such a degree that if you stick a pin in a leaf and then in a dog, the dog drops dead on the spot."

But her visit to Upsala was not equally interesting in all respects. "I was invited to look round the academy and was present at the graduation of fifty magisters, which, in truth, was not very entertaining, as the

103

ceremony lasted from 11 a.m. until 4 p.m. I must confess, that towards the end, I thought I would die of sheer boredom."

The collections that Linnaeus put in order for the Queen were to be found in the Naturalia Cabinet, some rooms further away on the same floor. In the "Museum Ludovicae Ulricae Reginae" there were, among other things "two very fine cabinets for naturalia" which the Queen had brought back from Holland, as well as herbaria from America, Egypt and Palestine as well as Kalm's collection of insects and butterflies from America. They were supplemented by King Adolf Fredrik's museum, brought from Ulriksdal, which contained skeletons, animals, fish in spirit and other objects. The collection was of high quality. Linnaeus wrote: "I doubt if any collection in the world is comparable to this one."

The Queen wrote the following about her acquisitions: "The collection of butterflies and other insects from India is very beautiful and the collection of shells is very comprehensive. I find pleasure in putting them in order along with a professor from Upsala, who is a great expert and scientist. He is very amusing and possesses the wit of the world without its other ways and on account of these two reasons I amuse myself greatly. Of an evening, he takes a stroll with the King and not a day goes by but he finds something to put us all in good humour." In another letter she says of Linnaeus, that he is "very interesting and clever, but one has to overlook the fact that he is a little boorish."

Linnaeus received gifts from the Royal Family, was created a nobleman and a Knight of the Order of the Pole Star, "a grace", he writes "which has never before been bestowed upon a professor". But he never became a courtier. "At Court, they never ask if one's clothes keep one warm, but about their cut and, if they are new, they are by this token, good." He also says about life at Court: "A whisper here, a whisper there, flattery, hypocrisy, lying, fawning, dauncing, singing." And he notes, rather drastically: "A lady farted at Court, paled, grew sick, went home and died. A Dutch seaman would not even notice."

The appreciation the Royal Couple showed for Linnaeus was based on the great interest, during the 18th Century, in the natural sciences. "Cabinets of Naturalia" were to be found at many of the Courts of Europe, such as those of Prussia and Austria, not to mention that of France with its "Cabinet d'histoire naturelle du Roi" in Paris. This was also reflected at Drottningholm in the cabinets for coins and mineralia. To get to these, you walk through the Marble Cabinet, the corner room where Lovisa Ulrica's library was originally situated. There then follow three cabinets, all facing North.

The Coin & Medal Cabinet, which comes first, is a pleasant room with panelled walls and areas with sculptured and gilded frames. It has the same measured proportions of the Library, but is somewhat closer to the Rococo in style. The Coin & Medal Cabinet was presumably

The oval Naturalia Cabinet with open door through to the Mineral Cabinet.

designed by Hårleman, but Lorentz Nordin's large showcase for medals, which ran along the walls, is now to be found at the Royal Coin Cabinet. The collections were based on the acquisitions of Tessin, bought by Lovisa Ulrica, and consisted mainly of "coins, medals, both symbolical and historical, jetons and tokens". It was bought by the Crown, but a proportion of the collections were interfered with before they were finally brought to the Coin Cabinet for safekeeping. A librarian at Drottningholm absconded with bags full of coins and medals. They were not found until 1853, deposited at the Bank of Sweden. But the aim was a noble one as I have already intimated. The embezzler wished to save his theatre at Bollhuset from bankruptcy.

It was in the Coin & Medal Cabinet that Lovisa Ulrica founded the Academy of Learning, in March 1753, and it had its first meeting on the 24th July, the Queen's Birthday, the very day she received the Chinese Pavilion.

Next follows the Mineral Cabinet which has direct access to the Royal Pew in the Chapel Royal. This was the last important piece of building work that Lovisa Ulrica had done. The room was designed by Rehn and the beautiful lintels over the doors to the Coin & Medal and Naturalia Cabinets depict coins, medals, coral and shells.

In the Naturalia Cabinet there are medallions with portraits of leading Swedish men of learning, made by Sergel. Carl Linnaeus is also among them. There is not much left of the collections. Two cases, made by Lorentz Nordin for exhibiting insects, are now at the University of Upsala. The splendid boxes made of card and covered in leather with the coat-of-arms of the Suedo-Prussian Alliance in gold, where plants were kept, are now empty. A few pieces of coral and a number of shells are all that remain of the Queen's museum, along with the crackled case of an Egyptian mummy. But one almost macabre item has survived. It is a life-size model of the dwarf, Bébé. He was the son of peasant parents from Lorraine, and was so small at birth that "he lay the whole of his first year in a shoe. He was usually clad in Polish dress or hussar uniform, was witty and intelligent and lived to the age of thirty. The dwarf Bébé belonged presumably to Lovisa Ulrica who had received him as a present from King Stanislaus". The 18th Century seems not to have been so enlightened that monarchs would desist from giving one another people as presents. As a counterbalance to Bébé, there was a cast of the hand of an Italian giant, Bernhard Giglio, who was "four ells, two inches tall", and had been shown to the Royal Family, in 1765. Another macabre feature was a royal foetus preserved in spirit. It was kept covered so as not to frighten pregnant women.

Unfortunately, the collections at Drottningholm were dispersed. In 1762, the coin collection was sold to the Crown and in 1803, the collection of naturalia was transferred to Upsala University. Many of the paintings are now to be found at the National Museum or at Gripsholm Castle. Many have demanded that the collections be returned. It has been maintained that if the scientific and cultural historical collections were reconstituted, then Drottningholm would "become a monument to the 18th Century, the likes of which could hardly be found anywhere in the world. The small amount of will power needed to get our learned institutions to send back their exhibits to Drottningholm, exhibits which are now of little material value, would be richly rewarded by the consciousness of having repaired a wrong, committed by a nation in a moment of impiety". "Barbarism" has also been mentioned. "Museums were founded, but one museum of exceptional quality was dismembered with great thoroughness".

I shall now leave Bébé, Rehn's interiors and books by Voltaire. I am retracing my steps, so as to continue on the floor above. But not before I have seen the Lower Gallery, or Charles X Gustav's Gallery, as it is also called, the long room on the lake side, with murals depicting battle

The dwarf Bébé in the Naturalia Cabinet was so small at birth that he lay the whole of his first year in a shoe.

scenes on the walls. To reach it, I pass through the Blue Cabinet, beyond the Northern Hall of the Lifeguard. It is a small room, originally the Queen's wardrobe. It has wood panelling and is completely in blue with flower garlands. The tile stove is made by Rörstrand, and is also in blue. The chandelier in silvered bronze is a purchase originally intended for the Royal Castle in Stockholm. The room is a concentrated and pure example of the Rococo. A leading art historian wrote that "this is one of the most charming rooms in the Palace. With all its intimate, tasteful ornamentation, it gives the visitor a feeling of the charm of the Swedish Rococo more than anything else".

Charles X Gustav's Gallery is a long room with a wooden floor and windows facing Lake Mälaren. The large murals depict, according to the captions, "Matters of war between Sweden, Poland and Denmark by our Royal Majesty, in glorious memory of King Charles Gustaf's victorieux exploits", and was painted by Johan Lemke, in conjunction with Erik Dahlberg. The paintings should give a reasonably accurate idea of what occurred during the wars against the Danes and Poles, as Erik Dahlberg took part himself. His sketches are also the basis of murals. Not least, those of the march over the Great Belt, Dahlberg also having taken an active part in that daring venture.

Carl Gustav Tessin admired Johan Philip Lemke who had been invited to Sweden to paint the large battle murals at Drottningholm. "The more that I see of Lemke's work, the more I am convinced that he is one of the most skillful battle painters we have ever had", wrote Tessin. But along with many more, Lemke discovered that Royal commissions were one thing, but payment another. Old and sick, he died in poverty and left two rings, a silver spoon and a cane-knob in silver. "He died, putting his epoch to shame, in most wretched poverty."

I am now back in the Lower Vestibule, and step out onto the splendid staircase. Both Tessins, the Elder and the Younger, contributed to its design. In Baroque architecture, special care was taken with the staircases. They were to be varied, lavish and as representative as space would allow. And at Drottningholm, the architects have succeeded. Lines, planes and the use of the various decorative elements, giving a living, rhythmic impression. The light, which emanates from three sources, adds to the whole.

Ehrenstrahl and Sylvius were responsible for the painting work, with Baroque illusion appearing in Sylvius' paintings of half-open doors which give onto larger areas, likewise his pictures of onlookers whom he sees on the stairs looking down from a fictitious gallery, modelled on Versailles. Everything is made to give the staircase a wider appearance.

The sculptor Millich, created the busts of Gothic kings on the stairs, but the Classical ideal was also alive. The goddess Minerva stands on the stairs in a niche and is considered to resemble Queen Christina. She is accompanied by two other statues along the balustrade. There is Apollo, the Sun God, who also stands outside the Court Theatre, and the Nine Muses. Both Minerva and Apollo appear again in the ceiling paintings, where Ehrenstrahl has them hold Hedvig Eleonora's monogram.

The staircase continues to the Upper Vestibule with a new parade of sculptures, busts of Roman emperors from Lovisa Ulrica's collection, which were placed there in the 19th Century. The ceiling painting was done by Sylvius and depicts "the world of the Gods and Olympus, here as small and well-fed characters".

The Upper Vestibule is also surrounded by Halls of the Lifeguard, the Northern and the Southern. They are richly decorated with walls of imitation marble, adorned with pilasters and cartouches. In the Northern Hall, there is a ceiling painting, again by Sylvius, where one of the angels has the wings of a butterfly. They do not seem particularly practical, especially for flying long distances.

In the Upper Gallery, Charles XI's gallery with its floor of Öland stone, there are also murals of the King's wars, by Lemke. A number of years ago they were restored, and none too soon. According to Carl Gustaf Tessin, they were damaged early on by damp which became rime-frost in the winter. Matters were not improved by a "wash which Miss Düben had them given, in 1719, when rough hands with the help of a little scouring sand took the edge off these otherwise incomparible pieces".

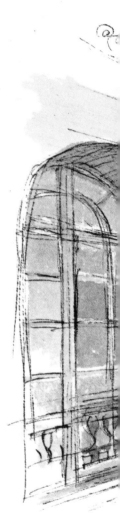

Gustav III also planned a gallery with battle scenes from his war against Russia. Desprez was given the honour, but the King died, in between. In the Museum of Maritime History, we can see those paintings the artist managed to complete. After the murder of Gustav III, Desprez' pension was confiscated and the brilliant artist died a pauper, was buried at the Church of St. Jacob but did not receive a gravestone. Only his housekeeper followed the coffin. The same tragic end as that of Lemke.

The Upper Gallery is the meeting point of the various components making up Drottningholm. From the lake side, I can look out over the rocky slabs of Kersö Island and the curtain of forest that rises above the waters of the Mälaren, glittering in the summer sun. And in the other direction, we can see the French Baroque Garden through the Olympian world of the staircase. The formalism of the Baroque, the Classical ideal of the Gods and the blond scenery of Lake Mälaren flow together in Charles XI's Gallery, under the heavy murals dating from a time when Sweden was a great power.

Nearest the Gallery, to the North, lies the Generals' Hall. The name is derived from the row of Charles XII's generals that lines the walls, painted by David von Krafft, Ehrenstrahl's nephew and his successor

Charles XI's Gallery

108

as Court painter. Charles XII hangs there alone in grim majesty, between the windows. The room is painted in dark colours and has a sombre, forbidding aspect. A mausoleum to the bloody Caroline era.

So far, I have passed through rooms where Lovisa Ulrica's light, pleasant Rococo and Hedvig Eleonora's heavy Baroque dominate. But where is Gustav III? Where is the Gustavian influence? John Böttinger, one of those who restored the Palace at the beginning of the 20th Century, and in charge of the Household, claims wrily that "his (Gustav III's) contribution to the early architectural history of the Palace was as unfortunate as his mother's were fortunate fortunate". He specifically points out Gustav III's alterations of the 17th Century style, where low, single doors are replaced by tall, narrow double doors. The ideal of the time was to see room after room, all in a row. Another case of stylistic interference were the wall-mirrors which clashed with the Baroque interior.

Böttinger's comments are perhaps not entirely fair. This can be seen from the Chinese Salon, a few rooms away, which was decorated by Gustav III. The walls are covered in light blue silk in a pattern designed by Rehn. The room is dominated by two such dissimilar items as a tile stove and a Gobelin tapestry. The tile stove, perhaps made in Petersburg and a gift to Gustav III from Catherine the Great, is a more original than a beautiful expression of the 18th Century fad for exoticism and chinoiserie. At Peterhof, Peter the Great's pleasure palace outside what is now Leningrad, I have also seen Chinese tile stoves in 18th Century settings, but not as decorative. The tapestry was manufactured at Gobelin in Paris. Many other so-called Gobelin tapestries were made elsewhere and sold under false pretences. This one is a gift to Gustav III from Louis XVI, when the former visited Paris, in 1784. It portrays Theseus who, according to Greek legend, killed the bull of Marathon and offered it to Apollo.

This tapestry is one of the most valuable items in the Palace. The gift can be seen as a political gesture at Royal level towards an important ally, rather than a personal gesture of appreciation. Marie Antoinette thought Gustav III clumsy and officious. Nor were other royal personages impressed by the Swedish King. Catherine the Great found him "theatrical", while Kaiser Joseph of Austria, writing to his brother about the King whom he had met in Pisa during the latter's Italian journey, said that he was "a man without character, false, with superficial *politure d'esprit* and education". His arrogance was insupportable and the King was described as "a swaggering snob".

The Blue Drawing Room next door is another example of Gustavian interior design. Elias Martin painted the lintels and the magnificent cupboard was made by Stenström. It has inlaid panels depicting the manufacture of silk and was constructed for the storage of silk samples. In the area of the Palace grounds named Canton, Lovisa Ulrica had set

110

A detail from the suite of tapestries depicting Hero and Leander. They were a gift from Johan Oxenstierna to Charles X Gustav, "the most valuable gift a Swede has ever given his King".

up a silk spinnery and mulberry bushes were planted for the sake of the caterpillars. It proved to be no more than an optimistic fancy, but Stenström's naturalia cupboard remains as do the colourful samples of silk. The cupboard also features in the work of Bellman, the renowned composer and singer of ballads.

Later kings have also lent their personal touch to Drottningholm. The Hall of King Oscar is one example and at the southern end of the upper floor lies the Hall of State, where Lovisa Ulrica and Adolf Fredrik's brilliant nuptials took place. It was restored by Oscar I in a somewhat hard-handed and insensitive manner. The breach of style is quite evident. Chaveau's and Sylvius' splendid Baroque ceiling piles up its dark masses of cloud over a room decorated in white and gold, by the 19th Century architect, Scholander. If you look closely you will discover a number of capercaillies on the parapet of the Greek temple.

On the walls of the *Galérie Contemporaine*, as the Hall of State was also known, are the assembled portraits of the European monarchs at the time of Oscar I. The walls are filled with portraits as elegant as postcards, of princes long since dead from monarchies long since vanished under the wheels of history. A unique row of Kings and Queens from Denmark, England and Spain along with their counterparts from Sardinia, Saxony, Bavaria and Würtemberg. I almost prefer the next room, the Queen's Hall. Here we find the masterpiece of the Golden Age of Swedish furniture craftmanship standing in solitary splendour, Georg Haupt's timelessly elegant Classically perfect bureau. Joséphine, Oscar I's Consort, hung portraits of contemporary queens in the Queen's Hall, a genuine Gustavian milieu. The paintings are surprisingly fresh, and I am struck by how beautiful most of the Queens must have been. But perhaps it was more like the caption under the picture of Gustavus II Adolphus in my history book' "Gustavus II Adolphus after a contemporary, presumably stylised, copperplate engraving".

I return to the Upper Vestibule by the staircase, and pass through the Southern Hall of the Lifeguard, the room which gives me the most genuine impression of the Baroque. The narrow, low doors. The massive open hearth which dominated the back wall, the broad boards of the wooden floor and the sculptured ceiling. The Baroque as a clenched fist of restrained power.

From the Vestibule, I can see over the gardens and the park. The Baroque Garden ought really to be seen from above to do full justice to it, to see the whole and to see connections in the geometrically structured whole. And I am struck by the importance of water as a decorative element. The cascades, and the fountains with their upturned waterfalls, glitter under the blue summer sky, giving life, tension and variety to the heavy, stiff Baroque. "Water and fountains are the soul of any garden", as Tessin, the landscaper of these gardens, said. The green lawns with their paths in black and red gravel ought really to be filled with winding arabesques of pruned box, but they are prettier without, giving a calmer impression.

When I descend the broad stone stairs, designed by the Tessins, father and son, I think of Johan Böttinger's common-sense philosophy for the restoration of the old Palace, when he removed some of the eccentricites of the 19th Century. He created interiors and milieux which, by way of furnishing, would "bring to the fore the total impression a dweller of the 20th Century would get of a room from the days of Hedvig Eleonora, Lovisa Ulrica or Gustav III". And he succeeded.

There are many rooms that I have got around to describing, there is a great deal of the Palace still to discover. I have kept to some of the rooms that I consider the most beautiful, the most interesting. But it is important to retrace one's steps. To wander at a leisurely pace through halls and salons. To stop and look.

My footsteps echo in the high stair well, or is someone following me? I turn around, but I am alone in the twilight. Minerva looks at me, marble-white, the inquisitive gaze of Sylvius' crowds look down at me over the painted balustrade. The sun has nearly set, down in the park. It no longer reaches up to the windows. And I think of things I have heard from some of the people who work here. About footfalls in empty rooms, shadows where there is no-one. A feeling of the "presence" of someone or something, where nothing can be seen. But there are many explanations. The wind, the old walls settling on their foundations, a shadow across the moon, out in the park. A twig rapping against a window pane in the wind. But who can tell?

So I go across the chequered stone floor and open the wide outer door into the evening sun, into summer. But it is not a historical monument, a dead, empty museum that I am leaving, as I gently close the door behind me. It is a living palace, filled with memories, people and events. A pregnant silence fills the old building, like a faint and distant breeze from long ago, through state-rooms and halls.

The street at Canton, the most Swedish of idylls.

Alchemists and Gamekeepers

The Palace dominates the park. The Palace, the Court Theatre, the Chinese Pavilion in Rococo, these are all cornerstones of Drottningholm. But there are also buildings throughout the length and breadth of the grounds which, without being magnificent, have nevertheless got their own history and interesting features. If you continue through the Baroque Garden and beyond Muncken Rise, you will find a small road that leads from the Chinese Pavilion out towards the main road to Ekerö. It is called Kantongatan (Canton Road) and the area is called Canton, ten or so low, 18th Century houses with their green gardens. The area originally belonged to Rinkeby, one of the old villages on Lovö, but was bought in 1745 by Lovisa Ulrica the year after she received Drottningholm as a gift from Frederick William I. But this was not in order to create a dreamy idyll. Quite the contrary. The vital and dynamic Crown Princess wanted to construct an industrial community in the optimistic spirit of mercantilism. And this was the fashion of the time. Linnaeus travelled around Sweden by request of the Estates, reporting on natural resources and the possibilities of developing the country. Coffee and tea cultivation were discussed for Sweden and tobacco began to be grown. Every natural resource should be exploited and trade and handicrafts were to be developed and promoted. Increased production and reduced imports were the order of the day.

115

Between 1753 and 1765 buildings appeared along Kantongatan. The idea was to set up a manufactory. They built "a smithy for polished blade-iron, an ordinary smithy, a polishing workshop, a gunsmith's, a silk-stocking factory, a silk mill and a lace-making school". "Poor young girls and young men" were also to be given free training. It was an ambitious and unrealistic project which did not succeed particularly well, despite the fact that lace-makers from Brabant were employed to teach the art of Brussels lace. Even mulberry trees were planted on Malmen in order to cultivate silkworms and produce silk.

The silk mill stood where Canton number 2, a small house, now stands. Silk material and bands were made there by weavers from Lyons. They even attempted to manufacture silk-stockings. This was a manifestation of the constructive though not always realistic optimism of the Age of Freedom, an epoch that dreamed of producing coffee and pearls in Sweden as well as importing camels. Attempts were made to tame elk as draught animals. A tame elk was presented to Adolf Fredrik. The animal was installed, along with his keeper and his family, in a little house in the park and was a great attraction. In those days, elk were a rare feature of Swedish fauna.

It has been asked why the area is called Canton. One explanation is that a book about Canton had just been published round about that time which was also full of the newly awakened interest in the large and mysterious country so far away and the name was not gainsaid by logic as "China", the Chinese Pavilion, lay at the other end of the narrow road. And Canton was the port where vessels of the Swedish East India Company called.

The idea of Canton was a good one, but the costs made it an unrealistic project. Activity decreased gradually. As early as 1773, it was noted that "Canton is almost completely deserted which is why the Queen encourages people to move there and these people shall not be burdened by expense, but shall keep the rooms in a fit state". But Lovisa Ulrica was nevertheless able to hand over "five pounds of raw silk" to the Estates. To this was added a similar amount from the silk cultivation in Lund and the Estates of the Realm had made two "splendid pieces of material" which were given to the Queen and the Crown Princess, Sophia Magdalena. And at the Palace itself stands a naturalia showcase, made by Stenström, with intarsia in the doors depicting the manufacture of silk. The inside is designed so as to exhibit the samples of silk which have remained there to this day. So it is perhaps wrong to bemoan the failure of the project. We never got a silk weaver's shop, nor do silk butterflies flutter around the park at Drottningholm, but an oasis from the 18th Century remains and the splendid Gustavian cabinet still exists. Greater industrial enterprises have left smaller traces, when seen in a historical light.

After the "industrial" period, actors and other theatrical people

anton number 8

lived at Canton during the Golden Era of the Court Theatre. Canton 1 is an interesting example. It is a red, two-storey brick-built house with white corners and green shutters. It lies, bathed in greenery, its black chimneys sitting atop a chipped tile roof. The house was granted Christian Karsten, the opera singer, by Gustav III. He built a Temple of Song in the garden. This is still standing, red walls under a roof of green sheet metal with a weather-vane whose pointer is in the shape of a heart. Karsten's widow died in Canton 1, at the age of 95. Her granddaughter, Marie Taglioni, became one of the most celebrated ballerinas of her time. The lace-making school was housed in Canton 3. Charles XIV Johan granted it, some time later, to Desquillon, "the Acteur of the French Spectacle". After that, the 18th Century milieu deteriorated, as interest in the Palace and gardens diminished, but Canton was rescued in the 1930s, not least by the efforts of the renowned architect Ivar Tengbom, and it has now become a unique sanctuary on the edge of the park.

Nearer to the Chinese Pavilion along Kantongatan lie three houses called, consistently enough, Lilla Kina (Little China), Japan and Kinetten (La Chinette). During the 1750s the King's "gun-wielders" or gamekeepers lived there, responsible as they were for hunting-dogs and weapons. In the same house, though much later, another person would come and live. This was Elsa Beskow, the children's writer, and it is no coincidence that her characters Tant Grön, Tant Brun and Tant Gredelin (Auntie Green, Brown and Lilac, respectively), Farbror Blå (Uncle Blue) and her other fairy-tale characters lived in an environment that could be taken straight from Canton. As I walk slowly down Kantongatan and the morning sun rises over the foliage of Muncken Rise, Petter and Lotta have just disappeared through the garden gate, the door shuts behind Farbror Blå and Lilla Prick (Little Dot) is barking under the pelargoniae beneath a half closed roller-blind in a window with white lace curtains. A fairy-tale walk in an 18th Century environment.

Canton has also been the setting for the idol of later generations, Pippi Longstocking, for which it was used as the film-set. Lovisa Ulrica of Prussia, Elsa Beskow and Astrid Lindgren. An odd mixture, but they have all, in their own way contributed to our image of Sweden.

In actual fact, my walk in the southern part of the grounds should end here, at Canton, the idyll that was not always so idyllic. In the 19th Century it was written that "the area where Canton now stands was once so waterlogged, autumn and spring, that you could spear pike there. You could see unkempt clumps of trees that came right up to the marsh, some low hovels here and there among stones and bushes".

Beyond the Chinese Pavilion, up on the rise, fields, hills and woods take over, and on the hillside behind the Chinese Pavilion stands the old substation like a last cultural outpost before the "wilderness"

Professor Evert Lundquist, one of Sweden's leading painters, now has his studio there. Nor can I resist telling of the manor Lugnet (Calm) that lay a little way off, with a view of the water. It was there that the chemist and alchemist August Nordenskiöld tried to make gold during the 18th Century. And this occurred with the approval of Gustav III. He is supposed to have even given Nordenskiöld a large advance to develop a method of making gold and silver out of Swedish iron. But no gold ever came out of Nordenskiöld's "boilings of aqua fortis", the King grew tired and Nordenskiöld went off "to distant climes for noble philanthropic reasons... driven by ideals of freedom, which marked the beginning of the liberation of the negro race, joined a colonialist venture on the coast of Sierre Leone, where he died in 1793".

But this was not the end of the manipulations out at Lugnet. One of the favourites of Gustav III, the Royal Equerry, Munck, entered the field. Munck was a typical example of the King's favouritism. He is said to have been a "handsome stable lad, who had been dressed up as a royal equerry". He could "hardly talk without uttering carnal oaths and his hasty rise has made him extremely particular, and instilled in him complete derision for the honour therein... at the time of the coup of 1772 – he was 23 years of age at the time – he was cornet and page but the same year he became Knight of the Sword and Royal Equerry whereafter he rose to Baron, Count, County Governor, President and Knight of the Seraphim, this last honour having but reached his forty-first year..." Persistent rumour would also have him father to Gustav IV Adolf.

Munck did not make gold, but he forged Russian gold coins by order of Gustav III. The plan was to utter them in Finland to finance the war against Russia and thus sabotage the Russian economy, but the manufacture proved to be too expensive and in 1790 he went over to counterfeiting Russian notes. Munck also counterfeited his own notes out at Lugnet. He forged "Fahnehjelmare" claiming that this was a task he had received from the King. "Fahnehjelmare" were promissory notes issued by War Commissioner Fahnehjelm for the Swedish troops to make their purchases in Finland. In 1792 Munck sent nearly one hundred thousand Rixdollars' worth of false promissory notes to Aron Isaak in Åbo (Turku), Finland, who acted in good faith but was arrested when he tried to exchange them. Isaak told who had passed them on to him and Munck was summoned by an angry King a few days before the shot at the Opera on the 16th March, 1792. A month later he was sentenced to reimburse the amount, was forced to relinquish his titles, hand back his decorations, leave the country and change his name. Aron Isaak was completely exonerated and was given permission to settle in Stockholm.

It is maybe not so strange that there was, for many years, a living tradition which told of "ghostly figures in most fantastic costumes"

The Palace from Malmen

who wandered around Lugnet with large hats pulled down over their faces. If one made gold on the strength of advance sums of money and forged banknotes, a degree of anonymity was perhaps felt to be necessary.

Apart from Canton there is also one other part of Drottningholm that has a character of its own. It is Malmen, the area to the North of the Palace, on the other side of the road. As early as 1737 we hear of "a little suburb" at the other end of the garden with the "Royal Brewery down by the waterside, close beside it the magazine, which is a stone building covered in brick. The publican's dwelling made of wood, which is newly repaired, also lies by the water's edge..." A little above we find the Palace clergyman's and watchman's houses as well as a school and bakery. "But all the other buildings both large and small are so unimportant or in such a state of disrepair that they are not worth a mention."

119

At the end of the 18th Century the situation was different. "Among the above-mentioned buildings, special mention ought to be made of the Governor's Office, now decorated with free-standing columns, the chemist's shop, the household store and several others, with some that have been built by private persons, so that this side of Drottningholm resembles a neat and pretty village."

Gustav III had added to previous plans of regulating the building on Malmen. In 1782 he issued Drottningholm Malmen's "foundatory document". His idea was to divide up plots so as to "encourage useful and active traders by giving greater freedom of trade" and who would have "complete freedom for trade and handicraft". The letter of foundation also relinquished the rights of King and Crown once the plots had been granted, but any building on them had to be approved beforehand. And the King succeeded. Doctors, traders, publicans, court-accountants and master-builders as well as tile-stove makers, millers, blacksmiths, carpenters and many others.

The King had great plans for Drottningholm and Malmen. During one particular period, Drottningholm and Svartsjö formed a separate county with the Governor at the Palace acting as County Governor. Malmen was not granted its own city rights, but had equivalent status.

When crossing the bridge from the island of Kersö the first building on your right is the Dukes' Stable. This, like the Court Theatre was designed by Adelcrantz. But before I continue up onto Malmen I would like to say something about the bridge. The original way over to Drottningholm was by boat. It was the most natural means. Waterways meant access, and not only to Lovön. But the road network was expanded and improved. No longer did one depend on sail and oars to come out here. The main highway was used as far as possible then the ferry across the various sounds and bays. There were many ferry jetties throughout the waterways around the Mälar Islands. To get from Drottningholm to Stockholm you first travelled by road down to the inn at Loviselund. The ferry went over to Tyska botten on the Bromma side. Then you waited for another ferry at Traneberg. But all this took time and energy. And once again it was Adelcrantz who solved the problem. By 1780 his plan was ready. A bridge from Drottningholm to Kersö. A new bridge from there over to Nockeby. The ferry point at Traneberg was replaced by a bridge to Kungsholmen. The plan was approved by Gustav III, but the project was not problem-free. Hard winters, difficult ground conditions and, as usual, greater expense than estimated. The bridges at Nockeby and Traneberg alone on the new highway which "is some hundred yards over ten kilometres" cost nigh on 100,000 Rixdollars. While the bridge to Drottningholm was a pontoon bridge, the one at Nockeby was built on stone supports with spaces for shipping to pass through. The inauguration took place in 1787. The King opened the three bridges, all on the same day. Spec-

The Dukes' Stable, Stenvärdshuset and Malmen. A bird's-eye view from the island of Kersö.

tacles, ... illuminations and a comedy by Bellman, "The Inn", all took place on Kersön, and Desprez designed a temple as backdrop.

The bridges at Drottningholm and Nockeby lasted a long time but modern traffic and new demands required new solutions. In 1925 the new Drottningholm bridge was opened by the King along with the County Governor and Göta Lifeguards' Band and a year later the new bridge at Nockeby appeared. Later, the flyover between Nockeby and Kersön was built, which was considered a great technical achievement. But I do not know whether Gustav III would have approved. His idea of a bridge made the Palace appear laid out before the onlooker as you came down the hill from Nockeby. The façade rose up against a background of greenery. "At one and the same time you have a surprising and magnificent view of the splendid Palace of Drottningholm." Today, that perspective has disappeared, but it is compensated by other factors. The Palace now rises gently as you drive over the bridge towards Drottningholm. Framed by the green tops of the oak trees, it rises above Kersön. When at the centre of the bridge, its

The Chancellery on Långa Raden

highest point, you can see the Palace lying there before you. Around it the summer sky and the glittering water down below. For a short moment you hover between sky and water, gliding down towards the Palace. This is something Gustav III never experienced from his bridge.

To return to the Dukes' Stable by the bridgehead on Lovön, it is interesting to take a look at the house to its right, Stenvärdshuset, a three-storey building with basement arches which previously supported another building. This is thought to have housed Katarina Jagiellonica's and Johan III's Jesuits during the 16th Century.

122

If you continue along the road, you come to "Långa Raden" (Long Row), the administrative buildings on the right-hand side along with the Kavaljerbyggnaden (Gentlemen's Quarters) which contains living quarters. Next comes the Pharmacy. It is thought that Gustav III was responsible for its architecture. Then we come to the Chancellery, designed by Adelrcrantz, with a façade of Classical pillars. Next come the residence of the bailiff and Minerva.

Further to the West, along the road, lay the Barracks, now demolished, a two-storey building whose stables behind Långa Raden are all that remain. The Ambassador, Francisco de Miranda "Liberator of Venezuela", wrote in his diary about a visit to Drottningholm in 1787. He describes these Dragoon Barracks thus: "The odd thing with them is that there are ballerinas' quarters in the upper storey and we noticed how the dragoons served them meals and, one imagines, other requirements – what deucèd company! So much more so as at night the soldiers call those that so desire in from the garden . . . for a trifling sum."

The lax morals that prevailed at Drottningholm were clearly not limited to members of the Court. Hedvig Elisabeth Charlotte, wife of Duke Karl, who was to become Charles XIII, comments on the licence somewhat sourly: "The *mores* that here prevail are indeed as scandalous as can be, and of an evening the most unseemly liberties are taken in the park. The wing in which I live is so situated that without myself being observed, I can see and hear everything and am in a position to judge what occurs." It is only to be hoped that the good duchess was not all too shocked, as she stood there behind the curtains.

Behind the more official façade of Långa Raden, lies an idyllic area of private villas with features from both the 18th Century and later epochs. Part of the charm lies in the fact that it has grown over the centuries with no other control than that of good taste. It would take too long to describe each building but one of the most beautiful houses in the whole of the Drottningholm area is Loviselund, which is situated in its own grounds down by the lakeside on the northern side of Malmen. It was here that the ferry from Tyska Botten on the Bromma side used to arrive before the age of bridges. It was once an inn and has a well-preserved 18th Century interior.

Another of the houses is Svanteberg which was granted to the Physician to Gustav III, Sven Anders Hedin, who was also doctor to the Russian prisoners-of-war who were quartered at Drottningholm. He was the great-grandfather of the explorer Sven Hedin and one of the pioneers of vaccination. Unfortunately, the original house has been demolished. At the top of Malmen stands Stora Klemmingsberg, built at the end of the 18th Century, by the "Aide-de-camp of the Corps of Infantry of the Burghers of Stockholm, Foreman to the Guild of Smiths", Johan Klemming. Up here Jean Meaurein planted mulberry

View from Långa Raden

bushes, to the joy of both the silkworms and Lovisa Ulrica. And here the bells of the Queen Dowager ring in the holiday from the old bell tower, over glittering stretches of smooth water and dark green foliage.

Not only 18th Century architects influenced the development of Malmen. Several leading architects of today have built houses here. Peter Celsing, who is responsible for much of the appearance of present-day Stockholm with such creations as the House of Culture and Sergels Torg, has designed a house that blends in well with the surrounding buildings. A more anachronistic specimen is Ralph Erskine's original house in stone and concrete. Many admire it, others see it as an example of what would have appeared more generally in the 18th Century environment at Drottningholm if some of the wicked plans of the more ambitious local government officials had not been thwarted, plans to turn Malmen's residential area into another Nockeby or Äppelviken which are situated at the other end of Kersön. While on the subject of original buildings, I must mention one further example. To the north of Malmen, near an ancient burial ground from the time of the Great Migrations, stands a large house dating from the 19th Century. It is the only Swedish house, that I know of, which has been in Rio de Janeiro. It was shipped there in kit form for an exhibition, but was not sold and returned, also by ship.

I continue my walk, leaving idyllic Malmen where *barouches* and *carosses* swayed forward on the muddy road on the way to the ferry at Loviselund, the road which is now rightly called Gustav III:s väg (Gustav III's Way). His "town" has changed its appearance. Millers, stovemakers and thatchers have vanished, leaving behind a sophisticated oasis for the upper-classes with a happy blend of the 18th and 20th Centuries which also incorporates the 19th Century joys of carpentry behind a screen of lilacs and rose bushes.

A little further along I come to the Governor's Residence. A large and stately house built by Gustav III and designed by the architect Gjörwell. Formerly, it was used by the Governor of the Palace, mainly as a summer residence, and rises up in a Iron Age burial ground, which has now been discovered. Unfortunately, the house has been cut off from its natural neighbour, the Palace grounds, by the highway out to Ekerö. This should have been planned in such a way so as not to destroy the balance of the surroundings. Now it in effect cuts Malmen off from the rest of the area.

The house named Vilan (Rest), is also cut off. It lies not far from the Governor's Residence. This fine building with its two wings, standing in a small park, was designed by Desprez and was granted for life to the balletmaster, Louis Gallodier. A caricature of him, with his long nose, is to be found on one of the walls of the Court Theatre. It is thought to have been drawn by Sergel. Vilan is only a pleasure palace in miniature, but it has had its moments.

The Gustavian façade of the Governor's Residence rises up over an Iron Age burial ground.

After the Gallodier epoch, other Court functionaries lived at Vilan. It was kept in good order the whole time and there were guests such as Jenny Lind and Carl Snoilsky. But the rot set in. At one point, Vilan was degraded to the level of a café and then to that of a laundry. In a room with Chinese wallpaper there stood two baskets of washing, water ran across the floor and steam hung around the old house like white smoke. But it was restored by the envoy Axel Wallenberg when he took on the lease in 1906 and Vilan was restored to its former Gustavian glory. Even Gallodier's old dining table with room for 36 guests was traced and put back where it belonged. Over the doors hang medallions by Sergel and the Chinese wallpaper, despite all it has been through, shines brightly on the walls.

But all was not pomp and circumstance at Drottningholm. When we talk about the Palace, its grounds and buildings, we should not forget the Crown Estate. Historically, the Royal Palaces not only had military and aesthetic functions, manifestations of Royal power and authority. There was also an economic dimension that was no less important. In the days before banks, financial institutions and share placement, land was the commodity that gave returns which one literally lived on. This was also the case with kings and court finances. The Palaces often had large tracts of land belonging to it and the King and his Court moved from palace to palace, not only to make their appearance in the various parts of the land, but also to enable th·m to live for a while on local resources. Dividends on capital were consumed, to a greater or lesser extent. This was also the case at Drottningholm, where the Crown Estate still exists today. All in all, the acreage amounts to approximately 800 hectares (about 2,000 acres). Where the Governor's Residence now stands, there once stood the Queen's Barn. It was a building with wings. The barn, and the other economically orientated buildings, which were added in 1910, now lie to the West of the Governor's Residence. Next to the red barn, we can see the Orangery which was a market garden until only a few years ago. It was moved there in the 18th Century to make room for the present Wing of the Lord Chamberlain next to the Court Theatre.

I walk back towards the Palace. Cut across the "carrousel ground' where Gustav III's knights stormed forth against troll and Turk's head with raised lances on their foaming chargers, during the magnificent tournaments. I pass by Monument Mound. Out on the hillock to the left stands a small pleasure house, now somewhat the worse for wear. At one time it was used as a swannery. I used to go there with my children during the days before Christmas. Father Christmas lived there. If you knocked carefully on the door and spoke through the keyhole, then perhaps you got what you wanted for Christmas.

I am walking up by the Court Theatre, towards the Breakfast Lounge. Up here are four detached wings, originally built for the brothers and sisters of Gustav III. I have already mentioned the Wing of the Lord Chamberlain where I lived. It was built by Gustav III for his sister, the Princess Sophia Albertina. To the South lies the Queen's Pavilion, formerly Duke Karl's Pavilion. Oscar II lived there, when still a duke, and Gustav V was born there. A stone with a date, at the foot of an oak tree in the hedge facing the English Park, was placed there to preserve the event for posterity. Today, you need to know of its existence to be able to read the text. In the garden, a ninepin-alley was to be found and in the wing Drottningholm Court Theatre Museum with its unique theatrical collections is now housed, the collections mainly the work of Carl Gustav Tessin.

On the other side beyond the statue of Apollo, and nearest the Court Theatre stands the Hunting Pavilion, formely Duke Fredrik's Pavilion. During the 19th Century it was filled with hunting trophies, huge antlers of elk and deer. These were obtained during the Royal Hunts where Oscar II was especially active. On faded photographs from the 19th Century the King can be seen, clad in hunting gear, with his suite posing by the pavilion along with the small game they have shot. For a long while it was also used as a residence for the King's suite and for the administration of the Court Theatre. In the Chapel Wing of the Palace, Arne Beijer, the rediscoverer of the Theatre at Drottningholm, had his "residence of honour".

And so I pass by the Palace again, along the gravel paths of the Baroque Garden and come to the King' Meadow where Oscar II and his children planted an oak grove one snowy October day, many years ago. Down by the lakeside stands a pretty, romantic building in greyish green under tall elms and dark green foliage. Dreamy and forgotten, it stands there with dark canals meandering past with their white and yellow water-lilies, under overhanging branches. Narrow wooden bridges with green-painted iron rails arch over these canals. But this is no Gustavian temple, a pleasure dome for romantic meetings, but something as prosiac as a bathhouse. It was built by Duke Karl in 1792, and is the oldest of its type in Sweden, a Royal Bathing Pavilion in the style of a Greek temple. It contained eight bathing rooms with hot and cold water, each with its own bedroom. "For those who wish to partake of Sea Bathing, there is a flat wooden floor which can be lowered into the water." A complicated procedure seen through our eyes, with the Mälaren lying all around, but it became the model for many other bathhouses, where you could lower yourself into the water without risking the gaze of inquisitive eyes.

Up to the right, as I stand in the oak grove in the King's Meadow, lies Flora Rise with its white goddess. Up there we can see a touching feature in the landscape of Drottningholm, a small graveyard for dogs. Gustav VI Adolf's and Queen Louise's greatly beloved "Elsie", a little Pekingese, rests there alongside "Tusse", "Mentor" and "Pascha".

The old bathhouse stands forgotten and dreamy like the setting for a Chekhov play under the dark foliage of the alders.

Overhead the oaks planted by Sophia Albertina in 1768 sough in the breeze.

Nearby, Alphyddan (Alp Cottage), a two-storey house "in real Swiss style" used to lie. It had seven rooms and was built to Queen Joséphine during the reign of Oscar I. The King often came here, especially during the last years of his life. It is now gone, but it was a peaceful and welcome sanctuary for a sick and weary King awaiting death. "It is impossible to enter the building without feeling the still peace, an almost inexplicable satisfaction, so different from the wonder felt on encountering the Palace of Drottningholm itself."

I am leaning against the rough bark of the trunk of an oak, can hear the wind in the heraldic greenery above my head, can see the majestic oaks in the distance that seem to be ascending Flora Rise. They are from the time of Gustav III, have seen the Palace being built, have been the scenery for Gustav III's carrousels. Here in the space of just a few square miles of ground you have a cross-section of Swedish history. Iron Age graves by the Governor's Residence, the Jesuits' house near Stenvärdshuset. Lovisa Ulrica on a walk with her children to the Chinese Pavilion. The peaceful idyll of 18th Century Canton. Oscar I's flight from a noisy world to Alphyddan, with a view over both the carrousel ground of Gustav III and the grassy slopes round about me and the water where the Viking ships glid out to sea. Here Johan III's deer park lay, here Petter Fredag routed King Christian's Danes. Today the drone of bumble bees and the scent of lime blossom. The glitter of sunshine on blue water. White gulls above the copper of the Palace roof. I am standing under the oaks in the outstretched palm of summer.

A Little about Churches

On Christmas Eve, we used to go to the Chapel Royal at Drottningholm. Snowflakes fell white, heavy and soft over the courtyard in the twilight, enveloping, muffling. The dark roof of the Palace faded with the falling snow. From the rectangle of light of the half-open door organ music could be heard. The congregation stamped the snow off their shoes, entered under the high cupola, sat down in the pews, while candlelight twinkled in the clear eyes of children. Christmas carols rose towards the ceiling, which was modelled on the Panthéon. The scent of candle wax, of the hyacinths on the altar, of the forest green a Christmas tree by the entrance. Soaring voices ringing clearly against a background of organ music. A living chapel at the old Palace. But it was not the first Chapel Royal at Drottningholm.

Johan III's palace already had a Chapel Royal. His Consort, Katarina Jagiellonica, came from Poland, was deeply religious, a Catholic. Gustav Vasa had indeed put an end to the power of the Catholic Church in Sweden, and had, with the help of the reformer, Olaus Petri, introduced the "true evangelical doctrine". Whether this was grounded in religious fervour or in the wish of a prince to strengthen his secular power, is debatable. It is perhaps not too difficult to answer the question. Sweden, which had been bled economically by

The Chapel Royal in the North Tower was begun in 1696 by Tessin the Younger but was not finished until the 1730s.

129

the war against the Danes, had somehow to be set on its feet again. The Hanseatic League demanded large sums for its support, and Royal power had to be strengthened. The possessions of the Church, including its holdings in land, were confiscated by the Crown during an epoch during which Gustav Vasa, with as much right as Louis XIV of France could say: "L'État, c'est Moi." After Gustav Vasa had, in line with his policy, made Sweden a hereditary kingdom, he was succeeded by his son, Johan III, after a period during which his brother, Eric XIV, wielded the sceptre. Eric was deposed and murdered, presumably on Johan's orders. But this did not stop Johan, as well as his wife, from having an abiding interest in religion. It may have been under her influence that he contemplated the possibility of some form of co-existence of Protestantism and Catholicism. This was also stated in his "Red Book" which was a series of suggestions as to the order of service, having points in common with Catholicism. "He dreamed of a reconciliation between the appreciation of beauty in Catholicism and the teachings of Luther", a dream which was to come to naught as a result of the Upsala Meeting, in 1593, which was ratified by the Riksdag (i.e. Parliament), a few years later. At the Meeting, the Augsburg Confession was accepted formally, and all forms of Papism rejected. But a token of the sympathy the Royal Couple felt towards Catholicism can be seen in the decision to make Drottningholm a sanctuary for Catholics. There, they were active for a decade or so after the Jesuit School at Gråmunkeholmen had been closed down, owing to the ravages of the Plague in Stockholm. In Stenvärdshuset, a building on Malmen, there are cellar vaults dating from the time when Drottningholm was a "hotbed of Jesuits" and it is thought that these arches supported the building that housed them. Furthermore, the King put Lindö Manor at the disposal of the Franciscans. At Lindö, even the Papal Legate, Antonio Possevino, celebrated Mass in Protestant Sweden.

The Chapel Royal, during the time of Johan III, was not a large one. Surviving records speak of "eight men's and eight women's pews". The Chapel, which lay at the centre of the old Palace, took up both storeys. King Johan's Palace had several different owners, but it was not until the time of Magnus Gabriel De la Gardie, during the 1650s, that records which are still extant were kept. De la Gardie started his restoration work in 1653. The Chapel Royal was redecorated in Baroque style and ornamented with paintings and stucco work. The Mediaeval altar in the church at Botkyrka is the only item on the Chapel inventory that has been traced. Katarina Jagiellonica received it in exchange for other things from the congregation, but it was returned to Botkyrka on her death.

In the spring of 1662, the Queen Dowager, Hedvig Eleonora, began building the new Palace, the old one having burnt down the previous

Detail of the altar-piece

December. Nicodemus Tessin the Elder became Palace architect and the reason work could be started so quickly was that Tessin had been asked by De la Gardie to undertake restoration work on the old Palace. The plans were revised, the project expanded but the basic plan had already been thought through by Tessin. The Palace was also to have a Chapel Royal, but construction work was carried out chiefly on the main building. As the construction work at the Royal Palace in Stockholm and its Chapel divided resources, work was not started until 1696. Hedvig Eleonora was not at all pleased about the delay. In an impatient letter dated 1698, she made the demand that "the Chapel Royal at Drottningholm must finally, this summer, receive its roof and the remaining building work must be undertaken without delay". There was some logic as regards the delay, however. The Chapel was being built alongside the main building, which was given a higher priority.

On the 14th May 1696, building commenced, "this day a beginning made upon the work". The grey stone foundations were laid within a matter of eighteen days in June by two masons from Floda in the county of Södermanland, Per Larsson and Sven Johnsson. Their workmen also drove iron piles into the rock under the Chapel. The master stonemason, Mårten Falk, was responsible for the brickwork, and in 1697 alone, 62,700 bricks were laid. The chief of quarrying operations was Anders Brokamp while John Grimson covered the cupola on the roof with thirty pounds of copper which Hedvig Eleonora had had Tessin provide for the purpose.

By the autumn of 1701, the exterior of the round tower at the northern end of the Palace was finished. The building material had to be transported over the ice during the winter and by barge when the water was ice-free. Both bricks and planks were transported from Stockholm by skipper Per Olofsson, sand came from Fantholmen and Jungfrusund and sandstone was obtained from Gotland. But the interior was not yet ready. During the first few years of the century, work at Drottningholm was concentrated on getting ready the Royal Suite and the Baroque Garden. One result of the Great Northern Wars was a lack of money and resources. And this would last until work on the Chapel recommenced. In documents from 1724, we read that the Chapel "has the beginnings of a luxurious interior but work is not yet finished". But better times were at hand. Ulrica Eleonora the Younger, the sister of Charles XII, a deeply religious woman, was keen on getting the Chapel ready, and in 1728, work was begun under the leadership of Carl Hårleman. Symptomatic of the situation was the fact that in August of that year, thirty windows were delivered. The Chapel had thus stood windowless for over a quarter of a century. The work undertaken by Nicodemus Tessin the Younger was now brought to a conclusion. The roof of the Royal Lectern, the inside of the cupola, inspired by the Panthéon, the five galleries with their staircases and the decorations with capitals and mouldings. The floor, consisting of 300 brown and white sandstone squares from Öland, was laid and the Chapel was completed with a north-facing altar and pulpit.

At the beginning of the 20th Century, restoration work on the Chapel was started. This was brought to a conclusion in 1912 and the Chapel Royal was re-consecrated on Ascension Day by the rector, the Reverend Bruncrona of Lovö island congregation, in the presence of Gustav V, the Crown Prince, Gustav Adolf and Prince Wilhelm. Almost 120 years earlier, Gustav IV Adolf had been confirmed here and one grey October's day much later, Gustav VI Adolf received Holy Communion the same day he became King. Gustav V had been present at the service immediately previously. And at a light and happy ceremony, 26 years later, Mrs Lilian Craig became Princess Lilian of Sweden before the altar in the Chapel Royal.

At the end of the 1970s, another renovation took place which, among other things, resulted in a new copper roof and a partial repainting of the Chapel. The interior derives its character from the fact that the Chapel is round, built like a tower. The pews are arranged to conform with this shape. The arrangement gives a feeling of closeness and of belonging. The format gives the Chapel a certain intimacy, in spite of the rather pompous Baroque character of the pilasters and pillars, where the white and grey gives a cool and dispassionate atmosphere and a "chaste" whole. The only element breaking with the austere Caroline Baroque is Schröder's altarpiece in a frame of angels on clouds in wood and plaster. Hårleman is considered to have designed the frame, inspired by originals at the Palace of Versailles.

Another feature that is special for the Chapel and inevitable for any Chapel Royal, is the Royal Lectern. It stands higher than the other four lecterns and is approached through a door from the Naturalia Cabinet, in the main building. On the rail we can observe the monogram of Ulrica Eleonora. The organ, now restored, was ordered by Ulrica Eleonora in 1730, from Johan Niclas Cahman. He was a pioneer of Swedish organ building and only three examples of his work remain.

Presumably for practical reasons, the bells were hung in a bell tower separate from the Chapel. This was first erected on the large piece of flat ground to the South of where the Court Theatre came to be built, approximately where the Apollo Belvedere now stands, but was later moved to Flaggberget on Malmen. On the larger of the bells we find references to God and to the Queen Dowager. "Gloria, gloria soli Deo", "Glory, glory to God alone" in Latin and then in Swedish: "Anno 1699 hafver hennes kongl. Mayt Riks enkiedrottningen Drottningh Hedvig Eleonora låthit giuta denne klocka til tiem klocka wed Drottningholm". i.e. Anno 1699 Her Royal Majesty Queen Dowager Hedvig Eleonora had this bell cast as the bell for Drottningholm.

HERS – Hedvig Eleonora Regina Sueciæ. The Queen Dowager's monogram shines in gold over the gates to the Chapel Royal.

In those days, monarchs had to give expression to their religiosity, whether this was rooted in personal belief or not. The Church and religion played an important part, and in the rôle of the "Lord's Anointed", and in connection with coronations, the Head of State was of great importance for the spiritual life of the country. Architecture was also a matter of Royal interest. The power of the Crown and the standing of the Head of State were manifested in imposing buildings. At first, these monumental buildings, castles in the main, were of importance for purposes of defence, but little by little aesthetic considerations came into the picture. Chapels Royal were built, and churches in the vicinity of the royal palaces often received the King's blessing. This was also the case with Lovö Church, where plans existed at various times to adept the church in conformity with developments at the Palace at Drottningholm. De la Gardie considered restoring Lovö Church during his short period at Drottningholm and right up until 1925 the King had royal right of patronage over the congregation of Lovö. This meant that he had the right to appoint their vicar.

If you go along the avenue away from the Palace, out through the English Park, past Canton, you soon reach the church at Lovö. Like a stone ship it sails out over the billowing landscape of fields, a little squat, a little ungainly, like the Viking ships as they made their way past, on their way on the open Baltic. Initially, in the 11th Century, the church was wooden. The runestones in the churchyard, the oldest of them dating back to the 1030s whose text is in praise of a deceased mother, shows by its cross that Christianity came early to Lovö, although paganism remained as can be seen by looking at other runestones. The wooden church was replaced by a stone one which was built in various phases starting at the turn of the 11th Century. The tower, with its pre-Romanesque windows, and the western part of the nave are said to come from the 1080s, while the eastern part of the nave was built at the end of the 12th Century. A thorough restoration took place at the end of the 16th Century after the church had been struck by lightning and was described as having been reduced to a ruin. Its proximity to Drottningholm also influenced renovation. Nicodemus Tessin the Elder was consulted and in 1670 he made a plan for both the interior and exterior of the church, which was partially followed. Other traces of the Palace can also be found in the church, for example, the remains of frescoes by Johan Sylvius, who was responsible for many of the wall and ceiling paintings at Drottningholm. The pulpit, with its royal crown, was made at Burchard Precht's workshop, and was ordered for the church by Hedvig Eleonora. The new spire was paid for by Ulrica Eleonora the Younger, who also gave the decorations in the tower as a gift, i.e. a gilt cock, globe and royal crown. Gustav IV Adolf gave an organ in 1797, and other monarchs contributed to the ornamentation of the church. The most recent restoration under the

Lovö kyrka

ike a stone ship, Lovö Church sails out
ver the billowing landscape of fields.

leadership of Berit Wallenberg was completed in 1935, after approximately one year's work. Among other things, concrete pillars were put in place under the church walls so that the arches would not begin to crack.

There is a long inventory for the church, listing everything from the font in sandstone dating back to the 12th Century, to the altar cloth which Gustav V embroidered and gave to the church. Gifts from kings and queens, gifts from individuals. Silver, textiles, portraits. A group of crucifixion figures in amber from Danzig belonged to Queen Christina as well as a pietà in ivory. A gilded wooden cross was given by Count Carl Axel Löwenhielm. It is fixed above the hymn board near the pulpit. Löwenhielm was son to Charles XIII and his mother was a von Fersen. His career is an interesting one. Lieutenant General, Governor, envoy to St. Petersburg. Officer during the Finnish wars, as well as during the war against Napoleon in 1813–14, this time on the side of the tsar. And he was not only Chief Aide-de-Camp to his cousin, the later deposed Gustav IV Adolf, but also Lord Chamberlain-in-Waiting to his adopted brother, Charles XIV Johan, who became King as a direct result of the coup against Gustav IV Adolf.

Among the graves outside the church, there is a monument to Olof von Dalin. He was Gustav III's tutor when the latter was still Crown Prince, but also a writer and satirist, a talent which proved to be a two-edged one. This fact Dalin discovered when one of his plays, performed by Lovisa Ulrica's amateur players out in the Palace grounds, was regarded as a diatribe against the Four Estates. The accusations did not have any adverse effect until the coup d'état of 1756, when the King's supporters tried to augment Royal power. The consequences were dire and led to the deaths of several Royal allies. The architect Jean Erik Rehn, who designed some of the most imposing rooms at Drottningholm as well as a good deal of the interior of the Chinese Pavilion, designed the huge obelisk over the grave of the man whom Lovisa Ulrica thought of as a new Voltaire. The inscription on the tomb is in Latin and ends with a summary of Royal appreciation:

> May the turf lie lightly upon him
> who, through fine and noble jest
> lightened the Royal burden.

This is also the grave of Gustav III's tutor, the leading mathematician, Samuel Klingenstierna. At the funeral "not only the Royal Family were present, but also councillors, members of the Royal Household, leading members of the Academy of Sciences and many others. Deeply moved, Lovisa Ulrica and Crown Prince Gustav entered the burial vault and laid red and white roses on the copper coffins. Never have individuals been so greatly honoured".

In the churchyard there are many other graves. Here lies, for example, Claes Rålamb, Knight of the Order of Seraphim and a member of the aristocracy. He is, however, chiefly remembered for winning the tournaments arranged by Gustav III, once at Adolf Fredrik Square, in Stockholm, and once at Drottningholm. Along the walls runestones stand. "Thorgisle and Signjut raised this stone to Vik, their father" is written in runes on the one marked with a cross, not far from the spot where Carin Fock lies at rest. She died in 1931, wife of Hermann Goering, who was executed as a war criminal at Nuremberg. It is said that Goering occasionally flew up to Sweden during the Thirties and circled over the little church. Between Olof von Dalin's burial mound and the runestone that commemorated Vik lies her grave. Three human destinies in a country churchyard, far away from the care and bustle of the world.

Crown Prince Gustav attended von Dalin's funeral. As King, he was to return to Lovö Church, not always in daylight. The 18th Century was not always so enlightened as one is led to believe. In spite of advances in rational thought and the natural sciences, occultism and superstition thrived, even in high places. Secret societies and arcane

136

Jean Eric Rehn designed the obelisk over Olof von Dalin's grave at Lovö Church.

rituals arose, seances and spiritism were at the height of fashion. It was an interest also shared by Gustav III. The Physician in Ordinary to the King, S.A. Hedin, great-grandfather to the explorer Sven Hedin, has described one event at Lovö Church.

"The Secretary Royal, Björnram, along with one of his assistants, were the first to arrive by the front entrance and they were, in my opinion, the real actors in this farce. Once they had entered the church, they immediately shut the doors and produced various items that I could not make out. I then saw how they affixed fine strings of horsehair to the chandeliers, to which they attached masks which were sewn onto white material tied to white bands, and raised them up by means of the horsehair strings afterwards lowering them again. When this machinery was ready, smoke powder was strewn on the floor. Not long afterwards, the King arrived with five gentlemen, among whom I recognised the Royal Equerry, Munck, and the Secretary, Schröderheim. The church was quite dimly lit and the smoke powder was set alight. The observers took up somewhat awkward positions with

137

rapiers drawn. Björnram made the sign of the cross a number of times and mumbled mystical words, whereupon an assistant, who was concealed from view, drew up the mask with the white material like a shroud. This mask had the face of Gustavus Adolphus. It swung somewhat as it was raised and was then let down quite gently. The other phantom represented Adolf Fredrik, and the same occured as with the other mask. Although I had seen all the preparations, I cannot deny that this spectacle was rather impressive. When both the masks had been lowered, a powder, presumably lycopode, was set alight, and this burnt with a pale glow.''

Lovö parish has had many leading clergymen, and was often the springboard to new, higher posts within the Church. Much of the documentation from Catholic times has vanished, but the names of priests such as Johannes, Nicolaus and Peter in Loghe live on from the 13th and 14th Centuries, as well as those of later teachers of the Gospel. I am thinking especially of Johannes Martini, nicknamed Herr Hans, who signed the declaration after the Upsala Meeting, in 1593, when the Augsburg Confession put a definite end to Catholicism in Sweden. But perhaps he had his doubts, nevertheless. He was suspended from his post for thirteen weeks. There were still Jesuits at Drottningholm and many centuries of Catholic piety and tradition did not just simply vanish without trace.

There is a long and well-documented history of the exploits of these priests and how they rose to become bishops and professors such as Jacobus Zebråzynthius during the 17th Century who was Chaplain, Professor, Pastor Primarius and Bishop of Strängnäs. But we can also find records of the difficulties a priest could encounter outside the stony acres of the care of souls and administrative duties. In those days, members of the clergy were compensated by receiving the yield of the farm attached to the rectory and were themselves responsible for its maintenance and upkeep. It was simple and tough arithmetic where a skillful farmer in a rich, plainsland parish lived better than a poor parson in the backwoods with his thin, meagre allotment. And some of the worldly seed did certainly fall upon stony ground. A certain Herr Lars was to experience this when he took over from Herr Hans as vicar of the Parish of Lovö. All he could find in the stable was a one-eyed horse. The vicarage had a lock on the door, but no key. The chimney did not draw so the fire could not be lit and consequently no food could be cooked. The furniture was gone, the windows had served their time and that which was reaped where Herr Hans had sown was miserable. But Herr Lars was good with his hands. When he died, in 1634, he left behind him a large, prosperous vicarage farm with newly-built house and healthy cattle. How he succeeded with the salvation of souls is not, however, mentioned in the old chronicles. Perhaps his predecessor, Herr Hans, had better luck in that sphere.

One of Herr Lars' successors was Eric Emporagrius, who died iɪ. 1674. He became Bishop of Strängnäs and published a commentary on the catechism which displeased Hedvig Eleonora to such an extent that she had the publication banned. Herr Eric claimed in it that a man ought to reckon his wife among the most noble of his moveables (i.e. moveable possessions). Being regarded as a moveable was not quite the stern Queen Dowager's cup of tea. And Mattias Iser came to Västerås as one of Sweden's richest bishops. Charles XI often visited him at the vicarage on Lovö. Was this also on account of Bishop Mattias' famous wine cellar?

Ulrica Eleonora the Younger, who was deeply religious, had a vicarage built that stands in a grove a little way beyond the church. The old kitchen remains to this day. Among the row of clergymen who lived at Lovö as vicar, was Anders Frostenson. He became an ecologist before the word was invented and is one of Sweden's great hymn-writers.

In the transparent space above the pointed tower of the church swallows dart. Larks hang in the elasticity of their song over clean-blown acres before the Spring sowing has begun, field that were once steel-blue bays. The gold star of Olof von Dalin's obelisk glitters. A tractor chugs, children come cycling along, out of breath. Outside the thick walls of the church, life bustles, inside, all is silence. I sit on one of the pews, filled with the timeless peace of the quiet nave. Lovö Church, a piece of Sweden, a piece of Drottningholm.

Lovö vicarage

"Proud Conquerors of the Waves"

A black plume of coal smoke sweeps down over the glittering waters of Riddarfjärden from the straight funnel marked with a white anchor on a red base. The hull vibrates, a muffled signal is given and slowly the "Prins Carl Philip" swings out under the gilded towers of the City Hall in Stockholm, where the three gold crowns of the Royal coat-of-arms shine against a background of feathery white clouds, high in the sky. The water froths around the propeller, more signals are given.

The "real" way, the oldest way of arriving at Drottningholm is by boat. Water linked, did not divide. Through into Lake Mälaren people sailed or rowed, depending on the weather. The roads were narrow and poor if indeed, they existed at all. Travelling between coaching inns on potholed roads through dark forest was both time-consuming and uncomfortable. Even going out to Drottningholm by road was a considerable undertaking. There were no bridges. You were ferried across at Traneberg and Tyska Botten on the Bromma side of the sound. Gustav III was the first to have bridges built. On one and the same day

141

during the summer of 1787, he inaugurated bridges at Traneberg, Nockeby and Drottningholm. Not the same solid creations of today, in steel and concrete – the bridge from Kersön to Drottningholm lay on pontoons, but this was an improvement. Now, the old bridges are gone, the worn and winding ways have vanished.

Today, it only takes half-an-hour to drive to Drottningholm by car. You first meet the Palace by the lakeside seen clearly over the water as it was by Gustav III and other travellers throughout history. But if you take the boat from Klara Strand and glide slowly between the verdant banks, this is the same journey as was undertaken many hundreds of years ago. The buildings have changed. Most of what was there has now disappeared, and the land has risen, the woods have been felled, but the structure and topography of the landscape remain the same. The further you travel from Stockholm, the more noticeable this becomes. This has been the waterway of the Vikings, the highroad of merchants into the rich hinterland of the Mälar Valley where tar and furs, iron and copper from the dark forests of the mining districts awaited. Queen Christina's pleasure yacht sailed forth on the same waters and, from the deck of his ship, Jean Baptiste Bernadotte looked out over the pastoral landscape which fate had made his own. This is not only a cruise to Drottningholm Palace, it is also a journey through Swedish history and culture.

The waterways of this area have borne human beings since the times when boats were made out of hollowed-out tree trunks. Throughout the centuries, an armada of boats has followed, with both peaceful intent and warlike designs, but it was not until the 17th Century that communications became organised. A licence was granted, in 1667, for a post yacht between Stockholm and Uppsala. Three times a week, the journey was undertaken in both directions, carrying passengers and freight. Regulations also existed. Passengers were not to create a nuisance by smoking or drunkenness, and if the timetable was not adhered to, the shipping company could be fined.

The yachts became popular. The journey between Stockholm and Upsala by road could take anything between three and eight days, by boat it took no more than a day. Behind the project was Olof Rudbeckius the Elder, one of the most many-sided men Sweden has known. His field of knowledge covered just about every scientific subject. As a medical researcher, he discovered the lymph glands, and as a botanist he was a forerunner of Linnaeus. He was also an archaeologist, a scientist and the rector of a university. Rudbeckius taught mathematics, astronomy, architecture and many other subjects. He left posterity his masterpiece, "Atlantica", a treatise in which, using a combination of creative and analytical intelligence, coupled with a naïvely romantic patriotism in the spirit of the Age of Greatness, he set out to prove that Sweden was Atlantis, the cradle of all culture. Here, paradise had lain,

here, history had its roots. Mount Ararat, where the Ark came to rest, was the Åreskutan Ridge and Atlantis lay in Upsala.

In time, boat connections increased, even within the Mälar area. But there was one great problem: the wind. Sail was used, though if the ship was becalmed or if the wind was against you, the journey proceeded by oar-power. The larger the boat and the heavier the cargo, the more impractical things became. But a new invention was to revolutionise the world, and even transport on the Mälaren. The steam engine meant the beginning of a new epoch. If we are to believe the story, the discovery was made in the Tower of London. The Earl of Worcester was a prisoner of the Crown in that grim gaol. His meals were prepared in his cell block. The lid of his cooking pot became stuck. The steam from the boiling soup created such a pressure that the lid was thrown up high into the chimney. The Earl, "who was an observant researcher into the forces of Nature", drew his own conclusions which he aired in 1633 in a publication entitled "A Century of Inventions". Newcomen and Watt developed the discovery further, invented the steam engine which arrived in Sweden through the offices of two remarkable personages, Baron Edelcrantz and Samuel Owen.

Abraham Niklas Clewberg, ennobled as Baron Edelcrantz, was a man with a "peculiarly split life's work". He was "docent" in the history of learning and knowledge of Nature, wrote the forerunner to the Swedish National Anthem, "Du gamla, du fria" (Thou ancient, thou free), came to be on particularly good terms with Gustav III, and became Keeper of the Privy Purse. Edelcrantz was also the President of the Painters' and Sculptors' Academy, First Conductor of the Court Orchestra, Director of Spectacles, i.e. Head of the Opera, Chairman of the Academy of Agriculture and President of the Board of Trade, to name but a few of his positions of honour. He wrote a dissertation on "telegraphs" and developed the optical telegraph for Sweden, a form of telegraphy consisting of sending signals from high towers. He had a six-metre high mast erected on the top of the Gothic Tower, at Drottningholm. To the mast were attached a number of moveable arms which could be manoeuvred from the top floor by means of ropes. The first broadcast took place on the 1st November 1794, as a greeting to Gustav IV Adolf on his 16th birthday. A recruit from the "Optical Telegraph Corps" sent the signals from the Gothic Tower, while the "First Engineer of the Royal Surveyors, Herr Öfverbom", sat at Traneberg with a telescope and a codebook. By means of a similar arrangement to that at Drottningholm, he sent the greetings further to the roof of the Royal Palace in Stockholm. The roof of the Church of St. Catherine was also used for telegraphy.

But telegraphy was not Edelcrantz' chief occupation. On a study visit to the Continent, he obtained, and brought back, four steam engines and built the first steam-driven mill in Sweden. This stood where the "mediaeval" City Hall now stands, rising up in red brick. The mill was called a fire-mill, as it was driven by means of a "fire-and-air machine", i.e. a steam engine. But it was to end in disaster. "When the fire-mill burnt down" is an old saying in Stockholm, which is still used, even though people do not always think back to what took place one dark evening in the year 1878. The glow from the conflagration with its showers of sparks could be seen for miles, and attempts to extinguish the blaze almost turned into a festival with Charles XV, who liked to direct the fire brigade, taking charge of operations.

Not far from the fire-mill, Samuel Owen lived and worked. He came to Stockholm at the beginning of the 19th Century to assist Edelcrantz with his steam engines. Owen had previously worked for Watt, the inventor of the steam engine, and had settled on Kungsholmen, roughly where the Mint now lies. His mechanical workshop had, among other things, a steam-driven threshing machine among its machine-building projects, a revolutionary step forward in the history of agriculture, similar to the advance from scythe and stook to the combine harvester. Formerly, threshing was performed by hand, in threshing barns. A hard and inefficient method needing a large work-force. Samuel Owen made several great breakthroughs for Swedish industry. He was elected a member of both the Agricultural and

144

"The Witch of Stockholm", the first propeller-driven vessel on Lake Mälaren.

Scientific Academies. A many-sided person, he also founded Stockholm's Teetotallers' Association and helped to bring Methodism to Sweden.

But Samuel Owen's contributions to society did not merely embrace threshing and religion. He was also important for seafaring. The steamships at the beginning of the 19th Century were paddle-steamers. They had large paddle-wheels on either side, similar to those of Mississippi steamers. On large stretches of water this proved to be a rather impractical method. The weight of cargo and also wind conditions could cause the paddles to rise or sink too much in the water, in which case speed and manoeuvrability were affected. Owen "hit upon a completely different idea, where a wheel of a different dimension was placed at the stern of the vessel, lying completely under water, thus driving the vessel forward". As early as 1816, 20 years before John Ericsson sought a patent for his propeller, Owen built his first experimental ship, complete with propeller. It was called "The Witch of Stockholm". He also built other ships, such as "Amphitrite", which "aroused great interest during its passenger-carrying voyages on Lake Mälaren", as well as the first iron vessel in Sweden, in 1840. This was the "Samuel Owen", which could travel at up to 13 knots, which was very fast for those days.

In August 1818, the first steamer to ply the Stockholm–Drottningholm route was put to sea. Owen announced in the newspaper, the Stockholms Dagligt Allehanda that: "My vessel, run by a crew of trustworthy sailors, will until further notice transport parties for trips on the Mälaren, at the cost of around 25 Rixdollars per day, but if hired for twenty-four hours at a time the fee is reduced by 50%. Sundays are excepted, when the steam vessel departs twice from Riddarholm to Drottningholm, first at 6 o'clock in the morning, the next at 10 a.m. For this the fare is 32 s Banco for the first and 24 s for the second saloon, the two saloons holding a total of 40 persons." There was also access to "food and refraichissements".

This was the beginning of a new epoch. Two years after Owen's advertisement, there were four steamers on the Mälaren, twelve by 1830, fifty by 1840 and ten years later, the number had grown to sixty-seven. The upward trend continued.

At first, paddle-steamers were in the majority, and out at Drottningholm there is a picture of the Palace with a paddle-steamer in the foreground. Then John Ericsson's propeller appeared, forcing out the paddles. Business flourished, and a 25% dividend on steamship company shares was not unusual. More and more vessels came to be used and the networks increased, as did competition. From city and village, jetties and harbours the white armada put to sea under a plume of black coal smoke, carrying passengers, milk, eggs, horses, cattle and potatoes. It gained great importance for farming and the growth of industry, and made life easier, not least on the small islands. The boats were also a point of contact. People met, talked, ate and drank during the voyages. At Riddarholmen and Munkbron the vessels lay at anchor. The Balder, Gute, Vilhelm Tham, Drottningholm, Gripsholm and Strengnäs, to name but a few. And at Klara Strand, the Prince Bernadotte and the Engelbrekt lay side by side.

But the development continued. Just as steam and the propeller had revolutionised Lake Mälaren of the 19th Century, the railways and the motor-car were to drastically change the picture during the 20th Century. The time of the old steamers was over. They were no longer needed. The jetties on the Mälaren lay pathetically empty. One or two tourist ships remained serving as nostalgic reminders of an old idyll. But interest was reawakened and the boat traffic was brought again to life. The Stockholm–Mariefred line is plied by the lovingly restored "Mariefred". There are many other vessels, and traffic to Drottningholm has increased. Now it is mainly tourists; nevertheless, Lake Mälaren lives again. And old traditions are revived. In the late spring of 1984, President Mittérand of France arrived at Drottningholm by boat on his state visit just as his predecessor Poincaré had done 70 years previously, on the eve of the First World War.

The "Prins Carl Philip" gives another signal, which echoes off the walls of the City Hall, the fairy-tale castle in National Romantic style which, despite its weight, gives the paradoxical impression of lightness. Does this depend on its windswept position between heaven and water? To stern lies the Old Town and the island of Riddarholmen. Barbara Hutton's old luxury yacht sticks its white swan's neck out beyond the stone quay. A rare bird among the broad-hulled Mälar skiffs, it has been transformed into a restaurant, moored and fettered with iron chains. "Sic transit gloria mundi", the way of all flesh. But not entirely. The food is good and she is still beautiful and well looked-after.

The sharp, pencil-like spire of Riddarholmen Church sticks holes in the summer sky above the round tower of Birger Jarl, under its dome of copper, one of the oldest buildings in Stockholm. And on Helgeandsholmen, the recently restored assembly hall of the Old Parliament Building glitters in the sun, swelling like a *bureau* in Rococo style.

Here is the key to Sweden and to the Mälar Valley affording protection against marauding Baltic pirates and other perpetrators of villainy. Birger Jarl knew this when he built fortresses and barriers in the middle of the 13th Century, an activity which swelled to become the founding of Stockholm and Sweden's new capital. The Chronicle of Eric tells of this:

"Birger Jarl, the wise old man
let build the city of Stockholm
with skill and application
a house so fair, a city good . . .

It is the key to the lake . ."

For ships were obliged to pass through the narrow sound where
Stocksund lay, to reach the hinterland. Snorri Sturlúson wrote about it
during the 13th Century. "From the whole of Svithiód all running
water flows into the Loginn (Lake Mälaren), but this has but one
outlet and this is so narrow that many a river is wider." And merchants
came. The cog-ships of the Hanseatic League waited in the salt waters
on the other side of Stadsholmen. On the Mälaren came ships with iron
and other export goods which were unloaded and taken down to the
cogs, over the ridge where the old town now lies. The German merchants who came to dominate the new city called themselves "Merca-
tores Romani Imperii', merchants of the Roman Empire, when they
moved North to exploit Sweden.

The propeller vibrates, the bells in the tower chime the tune of St.
Örjan. Far above, St. George fights his fight against the gilded dragon
of evil. He looks out over Sergels Torg and Klara Church opposite
where Sten Sture defeated the forces of King Christian of Denmark at
Brunkeberg ridge, more than 500 years ago. The statue was created to
commemorate this event. Its position is also of symbolic value. It was
just here, on Kungsholmen, that a strategically important deployment
zone lay the scene of many battles and sieges throughout the history of
the city.

The snub-nosed steamer with its broad stern that swings out across
the bay is no beauty. It has none of the sleek, smooth lines of a clipper.
Nor does it resemble the aristocratic, swan-like sailing vessels. It is
more of a dependable matron than a nervously slender-limbed bal-
lerina. But the stretches of water of the Mälaren do not exist primarily
for the sake of sailing and the aesthetics of shipbuilding. The boats here
are functional. Beauty has to go by the board, has to give way to more
practical demands, as so often in Sweden. Though other aesthetic
dimensions exist. Shining, newly-polished brass. Dark brown gleaming
mahogany. Glass and porcelain which clink faintly in the dining-room
due to the vibration of the steam engine. Tender whitefish and chilled
wine.

To the left, or in sea terms, to port, the buildings rise up on Söder
Mälarstrand with its moored barges. The rocks appear grey and rug-
ged between the houses, giving the impression of a fortress. To star-
board, Kungsholmen island glides past. Boats and sailing vessels curt-
sey gently in the wake of the "Prins Carl Philip". A long time ago, most

The last steamship of Lake Mälaren?

147

of Kungsholmen was owned by the Greyfriars, who obtained the island with the Pope's blessing. In theory, they were meant to own no possessions. But the friars were not only landowners, they were also suspected of unseemly worldliness. This went so far that an inspector was sent by the Church at Easter 1480, to check that the monks were not spending their time on "sperbräkan", i.e. jousting or "torneghian", i.e. tourneying.

Before us, Västerbro bridge spans its arch against the sky, and to our left we can see Långholmen's green and rocky island. This was not only the location of the prison, now closed down, used for solitary confinement, it also has a more noble history. Engelbrekt pitched camp here during the War of Liberation in 1434, when he besieged Stockholm, and here Gustav Vasa trapped the Danes when he linked Långholmen and Kungsholmen with a jetty, blocking off the sea roads.

On the other side of the water lies Marieberg. It is now the metropolis of the Stockholm newspaper empire with the papers "Expressen", "Dagens Nyheter" and "Svenska Dagbladet" occupying skyscrapers where the Rörstrand pottery and the old artillery school once stood. The water has been cleaned up to such an extent that you can catch salmon by the Royal Palace, just like long ago. You can also swim in the sea and here at Rålambshov there is a large open-air swimming pool. When will it ever be possible to swim in New York's East River or near the Tower of London?

In the distance, the traffic aorta of Essingen Bridge curves gently towards the centre on its high concrete pillars. A good friend of mine flew between the suspension arches in a Mustang but such feats of skill have long since been proscribed. There are two islands here, Stora Essingen and Lilla Essingen, or Hessingen as they used to be called. Lilla Essingen especially, was a popular venue for day trips from Stockholm. You travelled here by ship or by rowing-boat. Bellman was often there and on Ekensberg opposite, at one of the many "Bacchi temples" along the shore. In one of his epistles we find a crisp picture of a trip on the Mälaren, which occurred many years ago, when he tells of "Ulla Winblad's voyage home from Hessingen on Lake Mälaren, one summer's morning, 1769".

>   Movitz, give a blast on your horn
>   For those who sail on board the boats!
>   "Hey, Olle, what's a bull cost?
>   Listen what they answer!
>   Here, where do you hail from?"

"Lovön we come from
with greens and herring
milk and shiny apples."
Movitz sinks his morning dram!
Billows swell charmingly...
Can you see Ekeberg? Your health!
Listen how the people sing.

And in an impressionistic summary, Bellman reproduces the Sunday
afternoon atmosphere of the trip with the dozy drone of bumble-bees,
once the murmur of voices has died away:

In a bower, round their glasses
Several lads together,
Raise their glasses higher,
One or two with outstretched legs,
Sleep most deep, already snore,
Rest their heads against a stone
On a flow'ry carpet.

Rocky cliffs, ground smooth by the Ice Age glaciers, glide past, as
well as the luxuriant green of the lilac bushes with 18th Century
mansard roofs sticking out among them. Out on a promontory stands a
pavilion with a red roof, like a lady with a parasol, a piece of forgotten
19th Century. After that, the villas of the bourgeois begin stretching
along the shore, each one of them with its carved decorations. A
mixture of pastoral idyll, National Romanticism and Old Norse sym-
bolism. These were the summer paradises for well-off Stockholmers
who wanted to get outside the city limits during the warm summer
months. They were called "country crates" as "not only did they not
give any profit, they also cost a lot to keep up, used as they were to
entertain friends from the city, who would not call by without partak-
ing of the more heady beverages from the cellar". But it was not only
the cellars of these "crates" that were emptied. Many an inn stood on
the way out to Drottningholm as Bellman noted as he sailed past.

'Struth, how many a Bacchi kitchen!
From every den smoke can be seen.
Cramptest corner
Fumes of fusel.
Smallest bridge bears laden beasts.

This makes you think of the description by Lars Forsell of the Stockholm of Bellman. "A dung-heap and a midden, rife with epidemics, crime and alcoholism." Even if this is slightly exaggerated, it shows us an aspect of the 18th Century which is easily overlooked after a couple of centuries of idealisation and "literary" distancing.

But the waterside taverns are gone. The sun no longer shines on green glass bottles, the quiet thud of ninepins under the trees has been silenced forever.

The journey continues towards Kersön – over shimmering mirrors of sea, 'tween islets, meads, fields the jolly voyage runs – as we can read in "Songs from a Steamer". In the yellow bridgekeeper's cottage, out there on Kersön, whose pillars on the western gable originate at the Great Hall of the Royal Palace in Stockholm, lived the writer, Hjalmar Söderberg as a child. You can see the house as you drive over the

In the yellow bridgekeeper's cottage on Kersön lived the writer Hjalmar Söderberg as a child. The pillars on the western gable originate at the Great Hall of the Royal Palace in Stockholm.

150

bridge at Nockeby. In the novella "Martin Bircks Ungdom", he describes the summers of his childhood. "But the most fascinating of all was the long bridge and the lake with all the steamers which, while still some distance away, began sounding their hooters, so that the bridge might be opened to let them pass through. Martin soon learnt to recognise all of them; the Fyris and the Garibaldi, the Brage which was never in a hurry, the handsome blue steamer, Tynnelsö and the Enköping, a brown steamer which people called a coffee-burner as it chugged in a way similar to that of coffee being brewed."

The Fyris, the Garibaldi and the Tynnelsö. The names are sheer poetry. Summer, sun, lilac blossom along the lake shore. The whirl of smoke. The muffled echoes between the rocks. The sun on the water, the wake, white against dark blue, gulls wheeling around the chimneys.

But the "Prins Carl Philip" does not proceed towards Martin Birck's and Hjalmar Söderberg's bridge, but turns into the inner fairway, the one leading to the Palace. To the left, near the Mälaren, you can make out a long pole with a small metal hat on top, standing on a bare rocky hill. This is Kungshatt (The King's Hat) and attempts to explain the name have been as numerous as they have been imaginative. One version tells of how the King, when pursued by his enemies, plunged, horse and all, into the water at this point. Only his hat remained. Another version tells of how, when Olav Haraldson was on one of his raids, a Swedish peasant came and knocked the hat off the head of the Norwegian prince. Not to speak of the variant which describes the mediaeval king, Eric Weatherhat, who, in order to literally get wind in his sails used to turn his hat around. Unfortunately, the real explanation is quite prosaic. Names ending in -hatt are quite common in the case of bare, rocky hills. The "King's" hat of Kungshatt was presumably an ancient navigation mark.

On the sound, under the cliff, there are three old villas with carved decorations, a white one, a pink one and a brown one just before the small jetty at Kungshättan, where the "Prince Carl Philip" drops its passengers with a good deal of signalling, backing up and churning foam at the stern of the ship. The seascape here is that of the archipelago. Islets and holms, rocks polished smooth. Then something shines yellow among the reeds and rocks. The Palace rises between Kersön and Lovön, almost unreal in the barren archipelago, like a different palace seen from a new and unexpected angle. The gable, with its tower, dominates and in the foreground stands the greyish-green romantically antiquated bathhouse that Charles XIII had built. To the fore, a motorboat raises furrows of white foam in the smooth, blue bay.

We pass by the steep cliffs to the right, where the soldiers of the main guard used to bathe, before it was considered to have become an *"embarrassement"* for the ladies of the Court. This was before the era of bathing trunks. A lady-in-waiting complained to Gustav III that a contingent of dragoons had bathed naked outside her window. Slyly the King asked whether they had been completely naked. This was confirmed. "Then how does my lady the Countess know they were dragoons?" And there lies the Palace, peeping forth from among the luscious green trees. The "Prins Carl Philip" greets Drottningholm with muffled sirens, children wave under the oaks of the King's Mead. Is it Prince Carl Philip greeting his namesake? It reminds me of an early morning in May sitting in my office in the Royal Palace in Stockholm with a nervously smoking Prince Bertil and a King who was coming post-haste from Mainau. He arrived home in time to hear the salute being fired on Skeppsholmen, a rumbling confirmation of the fact that a Prince had been born at the Royal Palace. Another blast on the siren, smoke drifting towards the jetty where white marble statues, with the Ancient Greek orator and philosopher, Demosthenes, in the foreground, stand lined-up in a welcoming parade, as smoothly we berth.

The steamer, with its "fire-and-air machine" was, not so long ago, a completely new and revolutionary addition to the quiet idyll, laden with history. Today, in another epoch, with the Palace situated under the approach lane for landing jet aircraft from every continent, the steamers have become part of that same idyll. And even if the form of boat traffic is a little different to what they used to be, Octavia Carlén's recommendation from the year 1861 still holds good.

"Travel there on a fine summer's day, and you will find it flourishing, even in our days. See how early in the morning one steamer after another lands here from the capital, laden with passengers of all classes and kinds, dressed for a holiday, each steamer having its own little regimental band on board. Now we hear the deep and wonderful tones of our folk songs, now a gay Strauss waltz, now the measured notes of a march, now a rousing patriotic hymn. And the steamers, proud conquerors of the waves with their plumes of whirling smoke; they ply majestically back and forth, constantly bringing new crowds, who long to escape the warm embrace of the capital and come out to the fresh, flowering shores of Drottningholm, so beloved of Stockholmers."

Or C.F. Dahlgren, the man who wrote "Mollbergs epistlar", expressed it more directly:

> What draws nigh? Lofö strand
> Steps forth in leafy garb;
> Greetings, o Mälar'n's bride,
> Let me kiss thy hand!

I agree with them all; Bellman, Dahlgren and Carlén. The best way to arrive at Drottningholm, the most pleasant and most "genuine", is by boat. If, of course, you have the time. But this you need anyway to enable you to get into the mood gradually and enjoy the "Palace by the lake side", to allow your stresses and strains to die away. For this is the way Drottningholm ought to be experienced, coming towards us across the water, growing more distinct among the trees as for those who lived long before us, in the depths of history.

The Days of the Bernadottes

The Swedish Revolution of 1809 resulted in the fall of Gustav IV Adolf. It also brought with it a new and vitalising link in the chain of Swedish succession. Gustav III's brother, Duke Karl, had indeed become Charles XIII when his nephew was deposed, but he was old and childless. A successor to the throne had to be found and, in the event, the Danish prince, Karl August, was chosen. But fate was to rob him of his throne. He died suddenly of a stroke, it was said. Malicious rumour knew better. The cause of death was not a natural one, the successor to the throne had been murdered. The perpetrator of the crime was none other than the Marshal of the Realm, Axel von Fersen, who had been Marie Antoinette's lover and had nearly succeeded in rescuing Louis XVI from the Revolutionary gaol along with his mistress. But the escape attempt was discovered and the Royal Couple were caught and sent to the guillotine. An equally grim fate awaited von Fersen. He was lynched in 1810 by an angry mob on Riddarhustorget in Stockholm without either the military or the constabulary lifting a finger to help him. This act of brutality, "with blows of cudgel, kicks and stamping on head, breast and belly", was witnessed by the Chief of the Garrison, Silfversparre, the Governor-in-Chief, Klingspor, the Governor, Adlercreutz apart from a battalion of Svea Lifeguards consisting of two

Sweden's Versailles among pines and rocks.

155

hundred men on parade. This may have occurred with the knowledge of Charles XIII. It had been feared that von Fersen was planning a Gustavian Restoration. It also gives an insight into the state of affairs in the Sweden of the time, economically weakened, the rightful king deposed, and Finland, which had been a part of the Kingdom for over six hundred years, lost to Russia.

A new successor had to be chosen and, after many complicated twists and turns, the choice fell to the lot of Jean Baptiste Bernadotte, one of Napoleon's marshals. History has its moments. The official candidate was Duke Frederick Christian of Augustenborg, brother of the late Karl August. Before the election took place, however, the electors wished to be sure of not offending Napoleon, who was still in command of developments in Europe. Charles XIII's letter was sent to the Emperor by courier, a young lieutenant by the name of Mörner. He had his own ideas about royal succession. Sweden's honour must not be lost. Finland had to be retaken and he wished to see the "fall and decline of the power of Russia". The man to do this was no well-meaning Danish prince. No, one of Napoleon's marshals, supported by the Emperor and the French army, would be eminently more suitable. Baron Carl Otto Mörner therefore contacted Bernadotte who was not entirely indifferent, and the links with Napoleon were underlined in propaganda exercises before the election. One document states as follows: "As far as our political situation is concerned, what power should we not gain by joining forces with the mighty Emperor! Should we adopt a Prince, who, to our great good fortune, enjoys the esteem and friendship of the immortal Emperor and is linked to him by ties of kinship, as PONTE CORVO is brother-in-law to the King of Spain, then we would in so doing ensure ourselves a greater part of the goodwill of the Great Monarch than we would if some other person were to appear on the Swedish Throne." Bur Mörner's judgement was based on false premises. Bernadotte no longer enjoyed Napoleon's confidence. In actual fact he was to turn against the Emperor in an alliance with England and Russia and instead of retaking Finland he took over Norway for the Swedes. But that is another story.

The election of a successor took place at Örebro in 1810, a sleepy town far away from the troubles and intrigues of the capital. With the help of a French vice-consul, who spread rumours far and wide of generosity amounting to the payment of the national debt, and using miniature portraits of the Princess of Ponte Corvo and her son on matchstick holders, the opinion of the Parliament was swayed. Jean Baptiste Bernadotte was elected successor to the throne on the 21 August 1810. The historian Odhner wrote: "It was indeed an Act of Providence that called him, born in a hut, a stranger from the foot of the Pyrenees, to take his place on the throne of Sweden". It can also be said that, without the help of a wilful lieutenant, a matchstick holder and a vice-consul experienced in matters of public relations, Karl XIV Johan would never have become King of Sweden. And yet it might have occurred nevertheless. In 1807 Napoleon had agreed with the Tsar of Russia to attack Sweden where Gustav IV Adolf had become allied to England against France. In March 1808 Bernadotte had been commanded to go through Denmark, invade Scania and take Sweden. But he also had Spanish troops under his command. These mutinied, the invasion was cancelled and when Bernadotte finally arrived in Scania, two years later, it was not at the head of an invading army but as Crown Prince Karl Johan of Sweden.

Karl XIV Johan and Princess Désirée preferred other palaces to Drottningholm, even though the Crown Prince lived there before he made his ceremonial entrance into the city of Stockholm in November 1810. The Queen's feelings about Sweden were relatively lukewarm, at least initially. She was "bored to death" as she wrote, and only stayed in Sweden for six months, travelling back to Paris in the summer of 1811. It was not until 1823 that she returned to Sweden, along with her daughter-in-law, the 16-year old Princess Joséphine of Leuchtenberg. She had difficulties, not least with the climate, and used to say in Paris that she caught a cold just thinking about Stockholm. The Queen too, not only Karl XIV, had led an eventful life. She was the daughter of a rich businessman from Marseilles and was when young engaged to Napoleon before he left her for Joséphine de Beauharnais. She then married one of his generals, saw the rise and fall of the Empire and ended up as Queen of Sweden and Norway.

Karl XIV Johan's favourite palaces, apart from the Royal Palace in Stockholm, were Rosersberg and Rosendal, which he had built on Djurgården, and it is perhaps understandable that Drottningholm, whose upkeep had been neglected, was not one of the palaces most frequented by the Royal Family. Drottningholm was pregnant with Swedish history, shaped by royal families whose branches stretched far back to include the princely families of Europe, while the erstwhile Prince of Ponte Corvo, by the grace of Napoleon, was a fairly new shoot on the oak tree of monarchic heraldry. Karl Johan turned his back on the past and regarded Gustav III as having been a "fool".

Karl XIV Johan did not only introduce a new dynasty but also a new style, a new fashion, Empire Style. The Napoleonic taste for antiquities of Imperial Rome was transmitted to Sweden. Just as Greece and Rome had left its mark on the 18th Century and the Gustavian Style, Napoleon's campaigns to Egypt and Italy influenced the Empire Style. Rosendal, which lay near to the Royal Castle in Stockholm, was completely decorated according to the new fashion. In comparison, the sombre Baroque rooms at Drottningholm must have seemed old-fashioned and uncomfortable.

But Drottningholm did not stand completely empty. Occasionally there were festivities there. The British Ambassador to Stockholm, Lord Bloomfield, described a visit by the Royal Family in the summer of 1823, when Crown Princess Joséphine had come to Sweden. First they visited the Chinese Pavilion. After that dinner was served at the Confidence, where the King made fun of the dining-table with its system of raising and lowering which clearly did not function as it should. Did the food get stuck between the floors?

Drottningholm was a popular venue for trips by people other than royalty. The poem "A Journey Out To Drottningholm, 1819" tells of the visit made by a number of young gentlemen and ladies, also to the Palace itself, which was open to the public:

> "Here I saw Cherubim and Seraphim on the ceilings,
> Here I saw, the like of which I have never seen,
> A plaster cast of Gigli's giant hand,
> Compare with which Sally Hederlin's was tiny
> Here I saw, My God! how wonderful Nature
> Knows how to create all kind of Creature
> Here I saw in wax King Stanislaw's dwarf,
> A suitable doll for Anna Westerberg"

Clearly, the Naturalia Cabinet with the giant plaster hand and the dwarf Bébé were more interesting than Baroque Halls and Rococo rooms.

It became a custom, not only among members of the Royal Family, but also among Stockholmers, to celebrate Joséphine Day out at Drottningholm. At first, the outings and festivities had taken place on the 21st August, the day Jean Baptiste Bernadotte was chosen as successor to the throne, but the King himself decided that it should be the namesday of his daughter-in-law, Joséphine, which ought to be celebrated instead. The custom lasted many years.

In 1829, celebrations were especially lavish. The day was celebrated "with such luxury, the likes of which Sweden has never hitherto experienced". Circumstances were especially convenient. A few days before, Désirée had been crowned Queen of Sweden and many coronation guests were still in Stockholm. By carriage and steamer, members of the Court, the Parliament, the Diplomatic Corps, the higher ranks of the administration and divers invited guests as well as other Stockholmers flocked to Drottningholm. The steamer, "Josephina", landed at 10 o'clock in the morning. After that boats travelled to and fro between Drottningholm and Stockholm the whole day through. On the shore crowds stood cheering, firing shots of greeting into the air, and in the evening a magnificent display of fireworks was given. "This sea of light was of an almost terrible beauty". Eight thousand rockets lit up the sky culminating in the Royal monogram complete with crown. On

a tightrope spanned high above ground level from the Palace roof
appeared Mr and Mrs Fourreaux, who "performed in various beautiful
and daring poses".

When the firework display was over, the King and the Crown Prince
went to meet the people and were received "with an enthusiastic cheer
and deafening calls of 'hurray'". The band of the regimental guard
played "Folksången", then the National Anthem, and the whole
assembled populace sang. The bard, C.F. Dahlgren depicted the festivities in the manner of Bellman:

> Every heart was heard to beat
> Out of gladness, joy to meet.
> Only uncle, aunt and papa,
> Little friend, cousin, son-in-law
> These names used though all thought
> That they were of common stock that day.
> Known and unknown shook hands free
> With one another happily.

159

Is that not in that high window
Joséphine looking down
On the pretty flower basket,
Being carried to the shore?
Boatswain let the salute ring out,
Lightning, thunder, crash upon crash!
And may echo after sing
Thousandfold repeating!

Karl XIV Johan was well pleased with his daughter-in-law, Joséphine, who was to become Oscar I's Queen. Through her the Bernadottes gained a link with the old princely houses of Europe. The Crown Princess was daughter of Napoleon's stepson, Eugène de Beauharnais, to whom Mörner had also, in fact, offered the crown of Sweden, and Princess Amalia of Bavaria. This meant that she was distantly related to the Swedish Vasa dynasty and Karl Johan had printed and distributed family trees which showed Joséphine's links with old Swedish Royal Houses.

Even though Karl XIV Johan did not take a great deal of interest in Drottningholm, he had built the "Marine and Economic Wings" to the South of the Palace. During his reign, this part of Drottningholm came to receive its present-day look. The Palace itself witnessed only few events, such as the Joséphine festivities in August or when guests came from abroad, such as Tsar Nicholas.

But lack of interest resulted in lack of upkeep. The rot set in. The Baroque Garden was simplified by removing certain of its features, the fountains dried up and the park became overgrown. Inside the Palace, the plaster crumbled, the wallpaper split and some of the effects were dispersed. "The walls began to crack in an alarming way, the plaster loosened, windows were smashed in various parts, stucco fell in chunks down from the ceiling and the wall hangings fell to pieces. Apart from all this, auctions were arranged now and again, where objects about whose value no-one had the faintest inkling nor cared to find out, were sold at knock-down prices."

It was not until 1846 that the turning point came with Oscar I. As Crown Prince, he and Joséphine had become attached to the Palace and he now began renovation work, partly using private funds. He paid special attention to the Hall of State which was in the worst state of disrepair. A portrait gallery was set up with European monarchs from the time of Oscar I. It was the Queen, who through her family connections persuaded the royal houses to contribute a score or so of paintings. Not everyone appreciated the renovation. Johan Böttinger, the Chief Curator of the Royal Art Collections who was responsible for the thorough renovation at the beginning of the 20th Century was of the opinion that the rebuilding of the Hall of State "had succeeded in

160

ruining the 17th Century character of the room once and for all, by adding mediocre royal portraits, Italian marble stoves and a modern parquet floor".

The Stone Hall became a memorial to Karl XIV Johan, with paintings depicting his great battles. Just as with Charles XII before him, portraits were made of his generals. There were also paintings showing some of his more peaceful activities, pictures, for example of Pau and Örebro, his place of birth and the town where the election of the King took place, respectively. The Royal Couple continued the tradition of painting famous Swedes, and fifty or so portraits were hung of "the most outstanding Swedish men and women in the fields of art, science and literature".

Many other changes were made, mostly concerning decoration and furniture where the austere Empire style, with roots in Rome and Egypt, grew more bourgeois, moving over towards Karl Johan and Biedermeier. The Palace was, after all, a home for the Royal Family, at least to a certain extent, and was adapted to suit the style of the time. A fine illustration of the Palace as a home comes from the time when Oscar and Joséphine were Crown Prince and Crown Princess. In one painting, which Joséphine sent to her mother, Augusta Amalia of Bavaria, we can see the Crown Princess in Hedvig Eleonora's State Bedchamber, the most exquisite room at Drottningholm. Surrounded by the heavy gilt Baroque interior she sits there in a comfortable chair with a cushion under her feet. The future Karl XV, at about the age of five, is spelling out words in a book on her knee. In a magnificent armchair sits a little baby prince and in the doorway stands Oscar, later Oscar II, flag in hand. A picture of bourgeois family life in a pompous frame from the Age of Greatness.

The Palace was also used for receptions. Oscar I, for example, received Scandinavian students in the summer of 1856. Cheers, toasts and patriotic songs were all part of one of the highlights of the Scandinavian nationalism of the time. The King gave a speech after the meal, an important speech on foreign policy in the region of Scandinavia. "Thoughts of the past heighten the joy of the occasion even more. Gone are the times when brothers of the same stock were armed with terrible prejudice and misunderstanding against one another; when sorrowful feuds weakened our strength and increased the might and arrogance of our enemies! Of all these sad and cautionary memories only honourable ones remain. The Nordic contenders have tested each other's strength and taught one another courage. The surest foundation for friendship is respect... Henceforth, war between us Scandinavian brothers is unthinkable. This ineradicable decision has been carved in the breasts of two Nordic Kings, in the hearts of three Scandinavian peoples!

One delegate wrote: "These words by His Majesty were followed, as

161

were previous speeches, by a storm of applause."

But Oscar I did not talk only peace. He was Commander-in-Chief of the armed forces and allowed Stockholm garrison to have exercises out at Lovön camping in the park at Drottningholm. He himself spent the night, the first person ever to do so, at the Chinese Pavilion, presumably regarding the Pavilion as a little more in keeping with field manoeuvres than the Palace proper.

His son, Karl XV, was not as interested in Drottningholm as his father. He preferred Ulriksdal which he had redecorated. The traces he left behind at Drottningholm were chiefly negative ones from the point of view of the Palace as a collection of sixty or so paintings by foreign artists was rehoused at the National Museum, works by Rembrandt, Chardin, Boucher, Ehrenstrahl and Roslin, mainly from the collection of Lovisa Ulrica. But not all the art purchases had been such happy ones. Gustav IV Adolf had had acquired Professor Martelli's large collection of Italian, French and Netherlandish art from Rome. The purchase was handled by Gustav III's art agent, Piranesi. When the collection, after a great deal of humming and hawing finally arrived in Stockholm in 1803, the King had in fact bought a pig in a poke. "One can imagine the surprise of those concerned when it turned out that the pictures were not only mediocre, not at all reflecting the talents of the brilliant names of the old masters, but also owing to inadequate packing had been not inconsiderably damaged on the journey." But the purchase could not be returned and the best had to be made out of a bad job, even though the majority of the paintings ended up in the vaults of the National Museum. Some were hung at Drottningholm.

Oscar II continued the decoration work of his father Oscar I, but neither were his contributions always appreciated by purist art historians, unsympathetic towards the mixing of styles, where "Oscarian" elements had been blent rather insensitively with the purism of Classicism and delicate Rococo. The following was, for example, said of the chaise longue and the plush armchair in the King's Study: "One can see that they are strangers who have lost their way." The fashion of the time was an unoriginal eclecticism of neo-Renaissance, neo-Rococo and neo-Classicism spiced with Oriental influences in the shape of divans, drapes etc. Some of the changes were more thorough such as King Oscar's Hall next to the Chinese Lounge of Gustav III. This hall was decorated in a style dictated by Oscar II who let the architect, Agi Lindgren create a specifically "Oscarian" Baroque framework for the suite of tapestries depicting scenes from the legend of Hero and Leander. They have their own story. The tapestries were woven for King Charles I of England, but Cromwell came in between, had the King beheaded and sold the tapestries which finished up in the possession of Johan Oxenstierna, presumably when he was the chief Swedish negotiator at the peace talks after the Thirty Years' War. They then

One of the glass doors of the Chinese Pavilion which Oscar II saved from decay and neglect.

hung at Tidö Castle, but were given to Charles X Gustav as a wedding present. They have been described as the most valuable gift a Swedish subject has ever given his King.

Between the windows hangs a full-length portrait of Oscar II, painted by Oscar Björck, who also painted the ceiling paintings in the great dining hall of the restaurant Operakällaren, in Stockholm. There was a stormy debate when the paintings were unveiled, as certain figures, modelled on a labourer and his wife from the county of Södermanland, were quite blatantly nude. This was not the case with Oscar II, who was portrayed in the uniform of an admiral. To solve the problem at Operakällaren, the King suggested that Björck could make the reeds higher.

In the Hall of King Oscar there are also some Baroque chairs, copies of originals at Mälsåker Castle. They are probably the most travelled objects in the Palace, as they were shown at the World Exhibition in Chicago as examples of Swedish furniture design from the end of the 19th Century.

The interior designers of the day did not always have the same sensitivity for continuity and the same consideration for subtle interiors and exterior as those of today. And why should not Oscar II set his stamp on Drottningholm as all his predecessors had done? This he did too as regards things beyond the walls of the Palace. In 1874 he planted 600 trees and shrubs in the Lake Parterre which became an English Garden so that the Palace could hardly be seen from the lake. Not until 1949 were they removed and the view from the lake was restored to what Tessin had intended.

Oscar I and Oscar II deserve a good deal of credit, but it was really with Gustav V and Queen Viktoria of Baden that a more organised and constructive phase was entered as regards renovation. Gustav V was born in 1858 in the Queen's Pavilion where the Theatrical Museum is now housed, and he was christened in Oscar I's Gallery. Present were Knights of the Order of Seraphim, members of the Government of Sweden and Norway, representatives of the Court and the Diplomatic Corps. From across the water the rumble of gun salutes rolled towards the Palace where the little Prince lay in the cradle of Charles XII with his princely crown to the right of him and the Orders of Seraphim and St. Olav on his left. Archbishop Reuterdahl christened him in Charles XI's font of solid silver and the Queen Dowager Désirée was one of the godparents. When King Carl XVI Gustav was christened almost one hundred years later, he was carried to the ceremony by his great-grandfather, at whose own christening Napoleon's erstwhile fiancée and the wife of one of his marshals had thus been present. It was a christening stretching over three centuries.

But Gustav V left his mark on Drottningholm in other ways than with his restoration work. In the romantic spirit of the time, the Royal

Family had planted oak trees to commemorate important events. There is for example, a stone plaque at the foot of one of the oaks in the garden of the Wing of the Lord Chamberlain. The inscription on it tells of how the tree was planted at the birth of Gustav V. And there are other examples, too. Down on the King's Meadow to the South of the Palace, between the Baroque Garden and the canals near the bath-house stands a group of "Royal" oaks according to one of Oscar II's "notes". The 30th October 1881, the King, Queen Sophia, Crown Prince Gustav (later Gustav V), Crown Princess Victoria and Princes Oscar, Carl and Eugen all planted one oak each in the meadow, "which hereafter shall bear the name King's Meadow". A plan was also drawn and we can today identify who was the "godfather" for which tree, 100 years ago.

I can see them down on the hillside. The King. Tall straight, enjoying himself. With a cigar in his hand. The ladies of the Court saying "oh dear" and "well, well" in mock complaint, their hands in their muffs. It was cold and it was snowing. Stiff adjutants handling people spades as if standing to attention. The King wrote in his notebook' "Will these oaks grow and bear fine crowns above strong trunks? God alone gives the growth, strength and beauty. But if my children and grandchildren, if God grant me such, enjoy the shade these oaks afford one warm summer in the future, may they let their thoughts wander back to the day in late autumn when the first delicate oak saplings were planted in the snowcovered ground of the King's Meadow, and let their thoughts rest on the memory of the father, mother and grandparents who planted the first trees there.

May their work be continued by generations to come. Such hopes crown the events of the day."

Oscar II need not have worried. The oaks are still standing and have grown. Under them it is not his grandchildren who are playing but his great-great-grandchildren.

The restoration work that Gustav V started took place between 1907 and 1911 when the Royal Couple moved in. While living at Drottning-holm, the King had his private residence in the North East Wing and that of the Queen lay in the South West Wing. The work was led by Professor Erik Lallerstedt and the Chief Curator, Johan Böttinger. The Palace was equipped with central heating and the windows were replaced in the old style with small panes. In a previous chapter, I described the décor and Böttinger's philosophy, which meant restoring as much as possible to its original state, creating the impression of one specific epoch. And he did not regard modernisation as an end in itself. "Why should a palace, which has a style of its own, change costume like a lady following the whims of fashion?" He did not therefore retain all the changes made by the Bernadottes with any great amount of piety. Among other things, he removed the Karl Johan Room in the

Stone Hall. And he based the interior on objects belonging to the State to avoid the décor being torn apart if the estate was distributed during Royal inheritance.

Gustav V and Queen Viktoria frequented palaces such as Tullgarn and Sofiero but, in time, Drottningholm came to gain in importance, not least when Gustav V became a widower. He stayed for ever increasing amounts of time at the Palace and by tradition Christmas was spent at Drottningholm. Many years ago, Count Lennart Bernadotte described a Christmas Eve at Drottningholm, where tables of Christmas presents were set up for all the members of the family at first in the Generals' Hall, then later in the Charles XI Gallery.

"At last grandma disappeared one last time into the Christmas room to see if everything was in order.

Then the doors were opened.

Grandma stood smiling happily in the still candlelight and waited for us. We quickly arranged ourselves in a long line according to age. The youngest at the front, the oldest at the back. Suddenly grandma rang a little silver bell, and like an angel of Christmas goodness, she rang us all in to join the festivities.

I shall never, never forget that sight.

We enjoyed those seconds of waiting and, as we passed grandmother, she showed us our tables where the presents lay prettily laid out and arranged, and within a moment we were busy inspecting and discovering. There were no actual packets as there were far too many and unwrapping them would have taken several hours.

The large room was completely silent for a minute or two. We were overwhelmed by everything that we could take hold of and see. Everyone then began to talk through one another, and grandma wandered from table to table with a still smile on her lips. Wherever she went she got huge hugs. The floor was soon full of toys and games, in one corner someone tried out a new gramophone with the latest records and I danced a wild dance around papa who had at the last moment given me a wonderful penknife with lots of exciting blades."

And grandmother was, of course, Queen Viktoria.

Gustav VI Adolf is the Bernadotte who came to play the greatest part in restoring Drottningholm Palace to its original state adapted for the exigencies of today. He not only loved Drottningholm as a residence but he was also very knowledgeable and interested in the restoration work from a scientific and historical point of view. Work began in 1950, when he ascended the throne and was finished the same year he passed away, 1973. The Palace was partially restored as regards the interior and the façades were replastered and repainted, but perhaps the most significant achievement was the restoration of the Chinese Pavilion to its former glory, and the transformation of the Baroque Garden and the English Park. The Palace architects during that period were Professors Ivar Tengbom and Sven-Ivar Lind who have skilfully and expertly contributed to the creation of the Drottningholm of today.

Although Gustav VI Adolf also lived for long stretches at Ulriksdal and at Sofiero, Drottningholm came to mean the most to him as regards the pleasure palaces and, like his father, he spent longer and longer periods at Drottningholm, the older he became. It was a home to him, something which Queen Louise also stressed. In a letter to her niece she writes about her first Christmas at Drottningholm in 1923: "We have spent a very happy Christmas here and really enjoyed ourselves. It is a wonderful house for children with lots of rooms. We play badminton in the ballroom and golf in the billiards room which is very large and has no carpet. Johnnie (Prince Carl Johan) has his train set in a long gallery. In another room there is a 'listening apparatus' (radio) and also a gramophone. We always drink tea in the 'Christmas Room', occasionally we play with the children after tea or play Mah Jong with Gustav's parents. They have become fascinated by that game, even Ingrid and Bertil play it.

It's such a fantastic old palace, you must come and have a look one day. The view over the open lake is so beautiful."

Many occasions and events have been held at Drottningholm. I have described several. The nuptials of Lovisa Ulrica and Adolf Fredrik, Gustav III's carrousels, Oscar I's Scandinavian student meetings. But in modern times too Drottningholm has been used to hold receptions. The 30th May, 1959, was one such occasion. The Royal Couple held a banquet for 850 people in connection with the 150th anniversary of the 1809 Constitution. I have personal memories from several occasions such as when the then Crown Prince, Carl Gustaf, one sunny summer's afternoon in June, 1972 received delegates from the whole world who had come to the United Nations Conference on the Human Environment in Stockholm, one of the few international meetings which have brought forth positive and lasting results, and the largest international event of its kind in Sweden. Or when the OPEC ministers landed en masse in helicopters from a sky heavy with rainclouds on the emerald green lawns in front of the Palace to eat lunch. Not to mention when President Tito, with lightly tinted hair and handmade shoes to match his magnificent uniform, wandered around the rooms during his state visit in 1976.

But the festivity I remember best took place one June evening in 1976. It had begun at the Opera where much of the best Sweden had to offer musically, from Birgit Nilsson to ABBA, had appeared before many European "Crowned Heads of State" as well as for the other guests who had arrived for the wedding of Carl XVI Gustaf and Silvia Sommerlath the next day. By way of a misunderstanding by Court officials, the future Queen had been left behind at the Royal Castle and had to be fetched post-haste to the Opera. Out at Drottningholm, the

sun was going down over the Baroque Garden as the guests arrived. We dined in the various rooms and danced in Charles XI's Gallery. Late at night, I stood on the stone steps of the palace to cool off. A blackbird could be heard in the avenue of limes. The June night floated between night and morning. Behind me music wafted over from the Palace mixed with the distant sound of falling water from the fountains. A memory of Drottningholm.

With King Carl Gustaf's decision to move out to Drottningholm, a new epoch was begun at the Palace on Lake Mälaren, Palace of Queens. This is the first time a Royal Family has decide to live permanently out at the Palace and this means that Drottningholm is no longer simply a museum. It is also the home of a young Royal Family who give life to the old stone house in the park.

During the time of Gustav VI Adolf the Chinese Pavilion was renovated. Here the Volière – the former aviary – can be seen.

The Palace that Became a Home

– Don't you remember when my watch broke, daddy? Prince Carl Philip says.

– You mean your Mickey Mouse one?

He nods and Queen Silvia smiles. Like a young girl with straight, combed-back hair as she sits there in her white blouse and a checked skirt. In her lap she holds the young prince and behind them a fire of birch logs crackles in the tall open hearth of the Stone Hall which Carove made in 1679 following the sketch drawn up by Tessin. He received 250 Rixdollars in copper coins for the trouble. The February sun shines pale through the window making chequered patterns on the splendid carpet which King Alfonso of Spain once gave as a present to Gustaf V. In a silver Caroline goblet dark red tulips glow and on the walls hang rich Delft tapestries, woven for the coronation of Queen Christina. If you look carefully, you can see a crowned letter C under the Royal Coat of Arms, right at the top.

The Stone Hall acquired its name from its floor which was laid in a chequered pattern in grey and brown Öland stone. In the days of Hedvig Eleonora the Hall was used as a dining-room and reception hall and there was a canopy in green velvet and silver. On the ceiling there are three flowery angels from the 17th Century, but they no longer glide above the Hall of Memory that Oscar I had made here for Charles XIV, filled with portraits with the head of the Bernadotte dynasty as the central figure. Oscar II's plush seating and divans are also gone. The three angels now look out over a modernised version of the Queen Dowager's drawing-room where the King now sits on a long, comfortable sofa and talks to his son. Crown Princess Victoria is at school and her little sister, Madeleine, is having her afternoon nap. Despite the tapestries, the huge carpet, the chequered floor and the imposing Baroque cupboard, the large Stone Hall is in fact a cosy room, filled with a warmth that does not merely emanate from the large open fireplace in marble.

– Drottningholm is a good palace for the children, says the Queen and the King agrees. That was an important consideration when we moved out here from Stockholm. Our children can grow up in a much more natural environment and can go to school along with other children. We are all really happy here.

And I can understand her. With the King Carl Gustaf as my guide, I have walked through the private wing of the Palace where Gustav VI Adolf used to live during his stays at Drottningholm. It occupies the southern part of the "Portuguese Quarters" facing Lake Mälaren, the tower whose ground floor used to house the kitchens and the West Wing which faces the Baroque Garden. It was here that Duke Karl and Princess Elisabeth Charlotte had their quarters during the time of Gustav III, Princes Eugen and Carl lived there and here the Guest Quarters were also to be found.

A great deal of love and care have gone into the children's rooms where light, colour and space are important dimensions. This is, in fact not remarkable in a palace of more than two hundred rooms, but, as the King points out, previous generations were not so considerate as regards children with their décor and furniture. Once upon a time, he says, in the olden days, royal children were treated as adults. They lived and were dressed as adults and had ceremonial and official demands made on them which must have been incredibly tiresome. And we talk about the inhuman upbringing that Gustav III and Gustav IV Adolf were subjected to which, however well-meaning it may have been, set a fateful stamp on their lives, one of which was cut short by the shot at the Opera, while the other ended in exile. The fact that the royal ideals of upbringing are passé, not least as regards the décor of the children's rooms, can be seen in the many concrete examples of ingenious solutions to architectonic problems which have arisen when an old palace has had to be turned into a modern home for a young couple.

– The difference between living at the Palace in Stockholm and out here is enormous, says the King. We lived very comfortably there but we were in a way squeezed in, between a museum and a 600-room monument to the State. Our residence was literally surrounded by a quarter of a square kilometre of flooring. But here we have got ourselves a home.

And that is the impression that strikes me immediately as we walk through the tastefully furnished rooms in light, discreet colours. Old, classically Swedish furniture design, mostly from the 18th Century harmonises perfectly forming a whole where all the different styles come into their own without any one of them dominating, all within the framework of palace architecture. A powerful, modernistic wall-sculpture between two windows is a daring and sophisticated feature of a room where a young Swedish artist gives a touch of 20th Century on the wall opposite, among the carefully chosen antiques. This is a home. An active, living home.

I think of the residences of previous royal families, out here at Drottningholm. Of the pompous Baroque of the Queen Dowager, the gilt formality of Gustav III and Oscar I's maroon velvet tapestries. All products of their respective times and fashions, but the forerunner who most readily comes to mind when comparing the present King and Queen's way of putting their stamp on "their" Drottning is Lovisa Ulrica. Especially her light-coloured 18th Century Library which is still intact.

– We've given our part of the Palace a modern touch, the King adds. Every epoch leaves its trace, but the restoration done recently was very careful and respectful of what had gone before. By the standards of today, things were pretty primitive in this part of the Palace. My grandfather only used the Stone Hall, the Dining-Room and one other study. The rest consisted mostly of bedrooms and storage space. The kitchen, the plumbing and waste disposal had to be put in order. But while we were renovating we found lots of interesting things. Ceilings, doors and murals, for example. These have been conserved and documented. And the funny thing was that we'd already thought about them right from the start.

– How does Your Majesty mean?

– Well, when we discussed what we wanted, it turned out several times that this was the same as the original solution to the problem. We wanted, for instance, to break through a doorway at a certain point. And we found a door behind the wallpaper!

– Drottningholm has been called the Palace of Queens. Does Your Majesty have a favourite among her predecessors?

– I don't know about a favourite, she says with a smile. But I've always been fascinated by Lovisa Ulrica. She must have been a remarkable woman. She was so many-sided. Interested in science, literature and not least in the theatre. And her library was magnificent. Furthermore, she added to the Palace and gave Drottningholm much of the atmosphere and spirit it has today. You only have to take the theatre. It was she who had it built.

– But it wasn't only queens who lived here, the King adds, helping himself to a walnut from the big plastic bag which Carl Philip politely offers everyone. Let us take Gustav III. He was responsible for Drottningholm's most interesting epoch. He meant a great deal for the cultural development of Sweden and he was a skillful politician. You can, of course, criticise his ideas, but the fact he had a gift for politics cannot be denied, even though his achievements have been belittled for long periods of time. Though research has often been based on diaries and other material written by his political opponents. And prejudice sticks. For many, he is still a superficial theatrical personage who shouldn't be taken too seriously. But I am of the opinion that he is the most interesting person who has ever lived here at Drottningholm.

– Which is the finest room of the Palace? Which room do Your Majesties like most?

A pause. The fire crackles. A glowing cinder rolls out onto the stone floor. The black labrador Charlie gives a snort, yawns and returns to his dozing in front of the open fire.

– Hard to say. The Queen looks thoughtful. There are so many fine rooms in the Palace. From small, intimate, tasteful lounges right up to stately halls and galleries. Every room has something about it, everything has its special charm. But perhaps the State Bedchamber is in a class of its own. It's a jewel, not least from the perspective of art history, almost unique, at least in Sweden. And then there's the Library, of course. A wonderful room.

– I don't know, says the King. The State Bedchamber is indeed stately, but I was very afraid of it when I was little. I always thought it was haunted and terrifying. And even so, I never saw it when it was painted black. No, I prefer the Hall of State. The light is fantastic there of an afternoon and the collection of royal portraits is unique. But there's so much to see. Take, for instance, the cork model of the temple at Paestum which Gustav III brought back from Rome. Fascinating.

– Has His Majesty any special memories from his childhood at Drottningholm?

– I don't have any clear memories from the time of Gustav V, although we celebrated Christmas out here. But I do, of course remember the Christmas as we spent it when my grandfather lived here. It was all very traditional. The tables were set up ready with Christmas presents and when a little silver bell was rung we could enter the room. And for a while we didn't have access to Haga. At that time the family travelled out here so that we would have somewhere to play. So I have known all the ski-slopes and woods around here for many years. And when I became older I used to go on long walks with my grandfather. That meant a great deal to me.

– Is nature important for Your Majesty, I ask the King.

In the southern part of the Palace live the Royal Family.

— Yes. Being able to get out early in the morning onto a ski track or to put on a track suit and run a few kilometres after a busy day is something I can't do without. And it's all so beautiful! The English Park and the Baroque Garden. The whole area. It's funny that when foreigners come here they are always surprised at how beautiful it is. That the Palace is so well-proportioned. Perhaps it sounds banal, but I think Drottningholm is wonderful and it's a great privilege to live here. To be able to take the boat down by the jetty and sail all the way to Solliden certainly contributes to the fact.

— Don't forget the woods and the countryside round about, says the Queen. That too is an important factor which makes Drottningholm attractive. The combination of park and unspoilt nature. We often walk along the hidden path beyond the Chinese Pavilion. And the little pleasure palace itself is a jewel. Then there are the performances at the theatre. I agree entirely. Living here is a great privilege. And it's exciting. History comes to meet us every day.

– Other royal families have lived here before you and made their mark on the house and the gardens. Have Your Majesties any ambitions in this direction?

The King laughs.

– Things were somewhat different before. And the Palace is in fact "finished" both as regards the outside and the décor indoors. But I sometimes wonder about the grounds. Grounds are never completely static. Trees and bushes have only a certain lease of life. A park may have to be renovated. We'll have to see.

Carl Philip is playing with his walnuts. I tell him how small he was when I saw him for the first time, not many hours old, but he does not seem to believe me. He is a big boy now. And I think of Ingrid Björnberg's "Diary from Haga and Stockholm Palace" where the King's nanny and later Royal Housekeeper at the Palace tells us of one of Carl Gustaf's first visits to his great grandfather at Drottningholm. The King could well have been as old as Carl Philip is now, perhaps a little younger, when he played on the floor with Gustav V. "There they lay on the floor, the almost ninety-year-old monarch and the light-haired lad who would one day become King, and played quite contentedly while the ladies of the Court and the Royal Chamberlain Boström 'with the big belly' much loved by the children, sat around on their gilt chairs with tea cup in hand, looking on." Was this in the Stone Hall?

The Stone Hall is the room in the Palace which the Swedish people know best of all. It was Gustav VI Adolf's "sitting-room". Here the Royal Couple have held press conferences and it is here that various TV recordings have been made for Christmas programmes in which the Royal Family have taken part. And Prince Bertil and Princess Lilian were interviewed here after their wedding. When I recently asked the Prince about his impressions and memories of Drottningholm, he replied that the finest memory he had of the Palace was just specifically his wedding.

"I must be the only one in the family who got married at Drottningholm, perhaps the only royal personage in general, not counting Lovisa Ulrica and Adolf Fredrik's nuptials in the Hall of State. But that was more of an affirmation of the wedding in Berlin. Princess Lilian and I didn't want a lot of fuss with our wedding and it was a wonderful feeling to be able to be married in the little pretty Chapel Royal among our nearest and dearest."

Prince Bertil remembers other occasions too, ones occurring further back in time. Christmas at the old Palace. how they came out by car on Christmas Eve. "Rolls Royce 1914." And how grandma, Queen Viktoria, rang a silver bell and opened the doors to a paradise of tables laden with presents.

The Chapel from the corner by the sentry

"It was a shame that we never got to open any parcels. But it wouldn't have worked, anyway. There were far too many of us."

But Christmas at Drottningholm over the years did not merely consist of distributing presents. People skated on the ponds and if the days grew boring, badminton matches were arranged in the Hall of State in which Prince Eugen took part with great enthusiasm, wearing galoshes to avoid slipping on the parquet.

"We played so that the prisms fell out of the chandeliers on the floor below onto the billiard table. But I guess the period for prosecution has expired."

"I who have liked good food from childhood, enjoyed Christmas at Drottningholm very much. The Court officials were away and we had the place to ourselves. The Christmas table was more English and German than typically Swedish. Whole roast sucking-pig was one delicacy along with Christmas pudding, oysters, lobster. Though it was a lot of trouble for the staff. The kitchens lay in another part of the Palace and they had to cross the courtyard across planks that had been laid in the snow. I remember how I once was standing at the window of the Stone Hall and saw a poor footman fall down on his behind in the snow while food shot in all directions. I thought it looked very funny, but at that age I didn't know any better. And I was, of course, afraid of ghosts. I never saw any unfortunately, or perhaps I should say thank goodness, but others have done so. My uncle, Prince Wilhelm, for example. After a night in one of the guest-rooms, he refused to ever set foot there again."

The glow dies away in the hearth. A telephone rings behind closed doors. We chat on the long sofa and I think of the difference between then and now. The pomp, circumstance and aloofness which were the hallmark of times with many other royal families at Drottningholm are gone. The stiff and pompus Court ceremonial of the Renaissance, the Baroque and the Rococo no longer exists. The exacting etiquette of the era of Gustav III has vanished as well as the ostentation of the times of Karl Johan, with his Empire style. I am sitting here one day in February with a young family, occupied with important and demanding tasks which the Swedish Constitution requires of them. Ambitious, serious and aware of the great demands placed on them, they do a "good job" doing teamwork for "The Sweden of Today", something which strikes a Swede living abroad. A worthy link in the long line of Royal families who, over the centuries, have left their mark on Drottningholm.

– Duty calls, says the Queen with a smile and goes to arrange the schedule for the "domestic duties" at Drottningholm for the week along with the Royal Housekeeper. Prince Carl Philip gives me another walnut from his bag and the King follows me out through the Billiard Room, formerly the Queen Dowager's "minor dining-room" and the beautiful room facing the park which Gustav III used as a reception room when he was Crown Prince. Now it has been adapted with care to form part of the residence of the Royal Couple. A living example of the concept of "tradition and renewal". The Royal Couple are also the first ones to choose to live out here permanently, but in contrast to many previous generations they have not made any radical alterations in the old Palace. A portion of the Palace has been altered discreetly to meet with the requirements of the family, rooms that were previously used by Gustav VI Adolf, while the magnificent halls and all galleries are open to the public as before.

"I think you will agree that there are few palaces abroad that match this one", says the King as we look out over the park through the high windows. "But you should approach from the lake side", he adds. "Enter through the magnificent entrance hall with its perspective. In doing so you in a way leave everyday life and step into history."

Slowly, I wander down towards the steamer jetty, turn and regard the pale yellow Palace under the dark-coloured roof. Dusk is falling. An old palace has come to life once more. The laughter of children can be heard where silence reigned before. Of an evening the windows are lit up. Drottningholm lives. The heart of my Sweden.

Swedish rulers

	Lived	Ruled
Gustav Vasa	1496–1560	1521–3 (Regent), 1523–60 (King)
Erik XIV	1533–1577	1560–68
Johan III	1537–1592	1568–92
Sigismund (Zygmunt)	1566–1632	1592–99
Charles IX	1550–1611	till 1604 (Regent), 1604–11 (King)
Gustavus Adolphus	1594–1632	1611–32
Christina	1626–1689	1632–54
Charles X	1622–1660	1654–60
Charles XI	1655–1697	1660–97
Charles XII	1682–1718	1697–1718
Ulrica Eleonora the Younger	1688–1741	1718–20
Fredrik I	1676–1751	1720–51
Adolf Fredrik	1710–1771	1751–71
Gustav III	1746–1792	1771–92
Gustav IV Adolf	1778–1837	1792–1809
Charles XIII	1748–1818	1809–18
Charles XIV Johan	1763–1844	1818–44
Oscar I	1799–1859	1844–59
Charles XV	1826–1872	1859–72
Oscar II	1829–1907	1872–1907
Gustav V	1858–1950	1907–50
Gustav VI Adolf	1882–1973	1950–73
Carl XVI Gustaf	1946–	1973–

Swedish Queens
& Royal Consorts

	Lived	Period as Queen or Consort
Katarina Jagiellonica of Poland-Lithuania	1526–1583	1569–83
Katarina Stenbock	1535–1621	1552–60
Karin Månsdotter	1550–1612	1567–9
Gunilla Bielke	1568–1597	1585–92
Anna of Habsburg-Steiermark	1573–1598	1592–8
Christina of Holstein-Gottorp	1573–1625	1599 as Regent's Consort 1604–11
Maria Eleonora of Hohenzollern-Brandenburg	1599–1655	1620–32
Christina	1626–1689	1632–54 reigned
Hedvig Eleonora of Holstein-Gottorp	1636–1715	1654–60 1660–72 & 1690 as Queen Dowager
Ulrica Eleonora of Denmark	1656–1693	1680–93
Ulrica Eleonora the Younger	1688–1741	1718–20 reigned 1720–41 as Consort
Lovisa Ulrica of Prussia	1720–1782	1751–71
Sophia Magdalena of Denmark	1746–1813	1771–92
Fredrika Dorotea Wilhelmina of Baden	1781–1813	1797–1809
Hedvig Elisabeth Charlotte of Holstein-Gottorp	1759–1818	1809–18
Désirée, née Clary	1777–1861	1818–44
Joséphine of Leuchtenberg	1807–1876	1844–59
Lovisa of the Netherlands	1828–1871	1859–71
Sophia of Nassau	1836–1913	1872–1907
Viktoria of Baden	1862–1931	1907–31
Louise of Mountbatten	1889–1965	1950–65
Silvia, née Sommerlath	1943–	1976–